BALANCING WITH BUNIONS

A Story of Untangling the Knots of Life & Finding
Firm Foundation by Returning to My Roots

Donna Sewall Davidge/Amrita

Balancing With Bunions
A Story of Untangling the Knots of Life & Finding Firm
Foundation by Returning to My Roots

Donna Sewall Davidge/Amrita

Special thanks to Dorothy Holtermann at Birth a Book (www.birthabookcoach.com) for coaching me through the publishing process! Thanks also to Robert Louis Henry for technical help and page layout.

From our demons arise
sweet nectar (Amrita)
sense your roots
there is a home inside you
return home
discover peace, love, contentment and connection
To earth and all living beings
This book is my gift of words to you, friend.

CONTENTS

INTRODUCTION

This book was created from many years of free associations that I have gathered in notebooks. The first writing from me is a poem my mother gave me many years after I wrote it at thirteen. I began writing again in the mid-1980s when I was living in Paris. My next effort at writing was the mid-1990s for my one-woman show "In This, Our Home" in New York City, based on my great-grandmother's life in Maine. I started in earnest to write again in 2003, compiling the handwritten essays piece by piece on my computer in a collection I called "Someday." The title came from the family story about me and my three-year-old pronunciation "thumb-day" and the later *someday* of looking for the shooting star of fame in modeling and acting that never came. As the title "Someday" was soon already taken by an actress for her memoir, my title evolved into Balancing with Bunions, even though some people do not even know what a bunion is! I sure do! (and you will now too!). The current title was born out of the metaphor of being highly challenged to balance in one legged yoga poses with my huge bunions (a boney protuberance on each foot) while coming back to my family roots for another type of balance. In yoga the feet in fact represent being rooted. The feet and the legs are the earth element in our body, the grounding force rooted by 72,000 nerves endings in the feet.

As a yoga teacher in the healing arts since the mid 1980's, I have told many stories in my classes. I like to tell stories to help people be inspired and changed by my words the way stories have inspired and changed me. A few students and fellow teachers told me I should write a book. Little did they know I had been at it for years. I have had students say they would like to have my words with them. I received some messages that my writing might help others. After reading an article I wrote about nature and yoga for a New England publication, one woman wrote me that she was inspired to lose a huge amount of weight by walking for breast cancer, pulling herself up from depression

1

to give back to others. (She worked in a gun factory in New Hampshire, the only job she could get, living in a basement so she could tend her elderly mother. She went from size 11 to size 4).

This book stems from the deep love I have for nature, from my childhood summers in northern Maine, and especially from my love for the family history. I first hoped to impart this love of these things through performing about them. Instead, it is shared through the uncertain adventure I tell here of taking on what was left of my family history by purchasing Sewall House. Next I wished to share the home and history others, offering there the healing and spiritual aspects of yoga that have helped my life immensely. Here too is the story of my search for healing/meaning that led up to the purchase of Sewall House.

Three years ago, I spent three weeks going to the rustic second floor of the barn at Sewall House, every day breaking the ongoing writing piece I had into sections on index cards. Taping the index cards up on the wall was my way of creating some pseudo-logical sequence in the words I had written. The story is not just mine, but the story of a house and my family roots, which reach back to my great-grandfather in particular, a nature guide to a famous American. The story is of interconnected things – as well as the healing power of yoga and friendships.

I would like to thank especially Maria Massei-Rosato and Nadja Waxenegger for their support, as well as my father and mother for making this story happen because they made me, which in turn made the story. I would like to thank Marie-Aude Preau, who did so much in supporting the beginning of Sewall House with her artistic talent. By her own volition she created the perceptive cover image for this book in 1997 with me and my mother cut out of a photo of our first group at the retreat, then adding the woods, lakes and young William Sewall image, as well as my image in lower left corner, overlaid in my Kundalini Yoga turban like a spirit combining with the spirit of the house. My book is dedicated to these people as well as to so many people who have contributed to the learning, changing and growing which is the life I was given. I think and hope I have lived a path of growth, which may offer some inspiration and insight for others to do the same.

DISCLAIMER - none of the people in this story are meant to be slandered or any way portrayed as anything than my truth and subjective experience, truly no harm is intended toward anyone.

Me at age 9, Theodore Roosevelt Plaque in Bible Point, Maine

Donna miller
July 10, 68
103   81
"Why"   Language

Why is life a hardship?
Why do people die?
Why is love unhappiness?
Why do babies cry?

Is the world so sacred,
Or just another cell?
Is the world a heaven,
Or is the world a hell?

Do we need such hatred,
Or is our love the best?
Should we hate all living man,
Or let him be our guest?

Perhaps the world is just a dream,
Or could it be so real?
Perhaps the world it could be changed,
To something quite ideal.

—*Donna Miller (later Davidge), July 10, 1968, me at age 13*
[Transcribed on following page.]

WHY

Why is life a hardship?
Why do people die?
Why is love unhappiness?
Why do babies cry?
Is the world so sacred?
Or just another cell?
Is the world a heaven?
Or is the world a hell?
Do we need such hatred?
Or is our love the best?
Should we hate all living man
Or let him be our guest.
Perhaps the world is just a dream,
Or could it be so real?
Perhaps the world, it could be changed
To something quite ideal.

—Donna Miller (later Davidge), July 10, 1968, me at age 13

Sewall House at various moments in its history.

THE LITTLE OLD HOUSE IN THE COUNTRY

The little old house in the country
  Is very sad looking to me
The window panes are missing
  There is no mother to be kissing
Because the mother is dead,
  That is a thought I dread.

The things that I remember
  Are the dogs, the horses, the cows,
But the thing that I remember most
  Is the old hay mows.
I remember the cats, I remember the rats
  And the old swimming hole.

If I were in the country now,
  I would ride horses you see
And one of the children in the country
  Could ride on the horse with me.

But I am not in the country
  And never will be again.
The little old house in the country
  Will still yet there remain.

June 18, 1933.

Written at age eight by Julia Yarnall in 1933.
*Julia Hackengerg Yarnall, mother of Vermont wind warrior
Annette Smith, by permission.*

Chapter 1
SIGNING THE PAPERS

"I have been impressed with the urgency of doing. Knowing is not enough; we must apply. Being willing is not enough; we must do."
—*Leonardo da Vinci*

It's impossible, said pride.
It's risky, said experience.
It's pointless, said reason.
Give it a try, whispered the heart.

I have heard that what you experience in the womb can have a profound effect on you. There is expected to be comfort in the womb, yet what if the mother is struggling with thoughts of not wanting the pregnancy, accepting it in the best way possible, a dichotomy that the growing fetus feels? While my mother struggled silently with an unplanned pregnancy, I spent (and imagine feeling from the womb her peace there) three months in my mother's womb in the place she feels at peace, the Maine woods, my growing fetus already sensing the contradiction in things.

What had brought me to this day in 1997, forty-one years later? What likelihood?

Departing Connecticut as soon as I could "Needs to get out of Connecticut, at least for a while" written in my high school yearbook—to college at my father's alma mater University of New Hampshire... still not far enough from the family problems; to California...not far enough; so to Europe...my restless self ending up in New York City in 1985, a place a searching soul could be lost in anonymity and pursue almost anything while experimenting with life.

In this little northern town of Island Falls, Maine, no one could hide. Anyone who wanted to could know anyone else's business. Soon I would literally be in the middle of it, in a house that had been the epicenter of a once hopeful Maine town. Island Falls was sad now, much more so than when I had spent my summers in the woods nearby with my mother. My mother would take us "uptown" to Island Falls from the lake to visit our Aunt Nancy, who lived in the big house in the center of town, Sewall House. Sacred, the house seemed, because my mother would never let us wander its large mysterious rooms and halls. We never spent the night, never got to see the bedrooms, which were waiting empty, unused but hoping for a tired traveler to come rest their weary bones there. The rooms were missing the energy of years gone by when the house had been full of visitors, children, laughter, and love. Though Aunt Nancy had always loved the house, she was unable to have children to fill it, her first pregnancy a botched experience for her tiny body that had resulted in lifelong intestinal problems and a barren womb. Her children had become all of us—her nephews, nieces, and the children of Island Falls. Sewall House resonated with echoes of the past even as she and her husband, Uncle Maurice, kept it up to date and well cared for.

In 1995 Aunt Nancy turned 100. Many family and friends flocked to her home, still relegated to the first floor, the house full again with visitors, laughter, and love. All were there to celebrate a life that had been lived as her parents had taught her. My great-grandfather, William Windgate Sewall, had told his youngest, hoisting her on his knee as he looked into her blue Sewall eyes, "Nancy, this house was built on honor." On her hundredth birthday, Aunt Nancy sat in the green leather chair where she spent most of her time these days, especially in the winter months, greeting guest after guest in the house built on honor.

She sat that day in the same place her father had sat years before, poring over the letters sent to him over a lifetime by his friend Theodore Roosevelt, now long departed, a man he had known since he "had the bark on"— before Roosevelt was a mature adult. My great-grandfather, nature guide William Sewall, watched his young friend become many things, including president of the United States. Many knew the man as TR, but to the Sewall family, he was Theodore, which conveyed the reverence and respect my great-grandfather had had for this young man ever since he'd laid eyes on him from the Sewall House porch. A weak, bespectacled college boy at the time, Theodore had been sent to Maine to experience what he had yearned for since childhood—nature, the great outdoors. Northern Maine, still a frontier, offered that. My great-grandfather, the first white child born among the Native Americans who lived in Island Falls, was a good man to spend time with. His entire life had been spent living in and learning about the deep woods of Northern Maine.

I, in contrast, escaped to cities—San Diego, Fresno, San Francisco, Dusseldorf, Paris, Tokyo, and New York—before taking the step I am taking today. I have traveled to some beautiful places, including Nepal, Machu Picchu, Ireland, Brazil, and Alaska, all part of my bohemian life, seeking adventures, life experiences, answers to that questions "Why?" At age forty-one I am not yet settled in my soul. Like many of my choices, buying this house is impulsive, irrational. I am once again doing something unpredictable with no guaranteed outcome. If not me, who? No one in the family wanted the house. The contents had already been appraised and prepared for auction. The family history, like the letters from TR had been, sold, dividing and diluting this small slice of American history, my history, the house to be put on the market. Even if someone had wanted the house, who would care to maintain it in a way that kept its National Historic Registry status? It would be a skeleton, a structure without the contents that gave it life—its blood, its breath; the external wood walls might be replaced with vinyl siding, the heavy historic windows replaced. This structure, on its granite foundation, so meticulously planned by the strange-looking but talented architect Mr. Pingree, whose photo, like most everything, had been saved in the house. The home my great-grandfather had built over a five-year period for his parents in the last of their pioneer days, would be changed completely, or, worse yet, sit uninhabited as it, like so many other old farmhouses in this area, disintegrated year by year for lack of care.

I am signing the papers, not through a traditional mortgage held by a bank; I might not have qualified for a loan with my income as a yoga teacher, so papers are drawn up by the local lawyer, My relatives agreeing to hold the mortgage. I have driven up to meet with all three of them—Aunt Nancy's "boys," as she called them—the three nephews who inherited the house, who took care of her so lovingly, coming to set her fire in the morning or serve her orange juice so that she would be able to die in the same home she was born in, the house she loved—Sewall House. (My mother's cousins Sam, Bill and my Uncle Don, my namesake, all in their eighties.)

Mine wasn't a logical decision. Many of them are not. I was the wild child, the least likely candidate to be doing this. I had, as my father put it, "left a perfectly good marriage" after acquiring a master's in nutrition with research on cholesterol in 1979 (graduating magna cum laude), then running off to Europe in 1982 at almost twenty-seven to pursue a modeling career that turned out to be less than lucrative. Now back in the US, as my father described it, "Donna is trying to make it on Broadway." Actually, I was pretty far away from Broadway, doing exploitative B-movies, tons of off-off-Broadway plays, plus a lot of extra work on movies (being a human prop in hopes someone might throw me a line, which of course only works about one-millionth of the time). Like modeling, my acting career was proving to be non-lucrative. Why I expected anything to work at this point in my life, I am not sure. But I always seemed willing to try.

The theater piece I created in 1995 was the story of my great-grandmother's life (the woman behind the man), titled "In This, Our Home," my travels and searching pointing me back in the direction of my roots. The house might not hold the answers to the questions of life I had been seeking answers for, yet the experience and challenges of reviving it might hold some. Who knew that "This, Our Home" was to become "This, My Home"? On this day, I was stepping into the uncertainty of the responsibility, willing to take it on, with as much fear as excitement, again experiencing that dichotomy I first encountered in the womb.

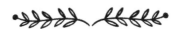

The ego is a monkey catapulting through the jungle.
Totally fascinated by the realm of the senses,
it swings from one desire to the next,
one conflict to the next,
one self-centered idea to the next.
If you threaten it, it actually fears for its life.
Let this monkey go.
Let the senses go.
Let conflicts go.
Let ideas go.
Let the fiction of life and death go.
Just remain in the center, watching.
And then forget that you are there.

—*Lao Tzu*

Aunt Nancy on a log on the lake as a young woman.

Chapter 2
THE SEWALL TREE

The Sewall Family Tree:
Much of this is from a Sewall genealogy website, with permission.

Searching Sewall genealogy reveals a lot. My family tree dates back to Coventry, England, including the *Mayflower*, some royalty and many strict staunch Puritans. Some of the Sewells and Sewalls are from the same branch, just one letter having been changed through time.[1]

Interest in my ancestry started with the immediate family tree, curiosity about my great-grandmother's life for the one-woman show. I glimpsed into her life through my mother's self-published book *Mary Sewall*, which was printed at a small shop in New Hampshire, sold at the Island Falls Historical Society. The one-woman show evolved from an imaginary discussion between Mary and me, with me asking if Mary's life and happiness could give me any insights into finding my own path. Mary's life was a pioneer one, traveling by wagon at age three from Canada to an undeveloped part of Maine, being instructed to leave her family at age twelve to become a servant girl, not for lack of love from her family but out of necessity. Had she been happy, I wondered? At sixteen, Mary was asked to teach a classroom full of children of all ages, some of them unruly. She developed migraines that crippled her. My great-grandfather, fifteen years her senior, first set eyes on her when she was a teacher. She married into the Sewall family at age twenty-one. William was thirty- six. The story my mother tells is that thirty-one-year-old William, who was driving by with his horse and carriage, was intrigued by the attractive young teacher clambering over a fence to chase a student. Five years later, he married the feisty lass. What was life like for Mary living with her

---

[1] http://www.sewellgenealogy.com/ui07.htm

mother-in-law and sister-in-law in the big white house I would own? The photos of William's parents, Rebecca and Levi, on the wall of the second floor landing at Sewall House show tight-lipped people who managed to live long lives despite the harshness of being pioneer founders of the Northern Maine town of Island Falls. I wondered what it would be like to meet them all now, in a time that would have seemed surreal to them.

I discovered writers on the distant branches of the Sewall tree. Oliver Wendell Holmes is a Sewall. Louisa May Alcott is a Sewall. I wonder if my mother knew that when she read *Little Women* to us by kerosene lamplight at the Maine cabin in the summer. Ralph Waldo Emerson was also a Sewall. Henry David Thoreau was in love with Ellen Sewall, whose father is said to be the reason she rejected him. This did not keep Henry from writing about about her long before he wrote *The Maine Woods*. Ellen herself was a good writer and daughter of one of the many Sewall ministers.[2]

One Sewall descendant, Jotham Sewall (1760–1850), a fervent Calvinist minister, traveled up and down the east coast preaching 12,867 sermons. When his daughter died at age two, her tombstone inscription read, "She hath sinned against the Lord." There is a long line of ministers in the Sewall family. My mother's language toward me as a young child came from the mouth of a descendant of these Protestant Puritans, their discipline a form of abusive language, their rationalized attempt at living what they claimed to be a godly life.

I find Mary Chilton intriguing, the only Sewall female who traveled on the *Mayflower*. The other two Sewalls on board were men, one of whom later killed another member of the colony. He was hanged for murder in 1630. The other, John Howland, fell overboard during a storm and survived by grabbing a trailing line that enabled a crew member to pull him back in. As the George Bushes are his direct descendants, if he had not survived we would have had no George Bushes as president.

Mary Chilton was orphaned before reaching Plymouth at age thirteen. She was taken in, the records say, by another family and became a servant girl. She later married John Winslow, who came to America on the *Mayflower* as well. Mary Chilton has many descendants. I imagine

---

[2] https://beforewalden.wordpress.com/2014/06/17/ellen-sewall-the-real-reason-henry-thoreau-went-to-live-in-the-woods/

her as the heroine of her own life, in a new country with no family, courageously finding her way, an orphan assisted by the kindness of others.

Another Sewall woman, who was ahead of her time, is Emma D. Crooker Sewall, a noted nineteenth-century photographer (1836–1919, the year TR died). She married a wealthy Sewall from Bath, Maine, where many Sewalls found success in the shipping industry. Her husband ran for vice president opposite TR when William McKinley was elected. Had Emma's husband been vice president instead, TR might never have been president because he attained the office after the assassination of McKinley. Emma's photography shows the stark simple beauty in Maine life, of workers in the fields, of families in sparsely furnished homes. After her husband died, Emma retreated into the seclusion of nature, much as yogis do after they have accomplished their work in the "outer" world. This included giving her cameras away despite displays of her work in galleries; her creation of art also retreated after her husband's death.

As a young girl, I had dreams of becoming the first woman president, naively thinking that all presidents performed great acts like Abraham Lincoln's freeing of the slaves. John Adams, our second president, and John Quincy Adams, the sixth president, are Sewall descendants, as is John Hancock, first signer of the Declaration of Independence. Judge Samuel Sewall of Massachusetts, whose notoriety came from convicting witches during the Salem witch trials, later repented, evolving into a civil rights activist, another Sewall political figure.

On my father's side of the family, I know little of the history except that my father's grandfather on his father's side was the oldest living Civil War veteran in Maine. Algernon fathered ten children, claiming he was "never sick a day in his life" after being left for dead on the battlefield. He lied about his age to go to war, then spent five months in a hospital recovering from near death. At age ninety-six, Algernon called my father to him— the first time he met my father Algernon was age ninety—and told my him, "Wilbur, life is just not fun anymore." Algernon was gone four days after telling my father those words.

I think my father would have loved the challenge and service of politics. He went into chemistry instead of law, as his college advisor told him that chemistry was an emerging field that would always assure him of a job where he could apply his gifted intellect and pro-vide for his family. My father was the (volunteer) founder of the Stamford Forum for World Affairs, which hosted such eloquent speakers as Eleanor Roosevelt, Henry Kissinger, and Barbara Bush, to name but a few. He also discovered two drugs, both being used today. Diamox is used by all mountain climbers for altitude sickness, among other uses related to the treating the heart.

***

"To be without a history is like being forgotten. My grandfather did not know the maiden name of either of his grandmothers. I thought that to be forgotten must be the worst fate of all."
—Donald Hall from *Message Through Time*

photo permission Frederic Silberman

One hundred and ten years before I was born. A speck in time. Two families forge the frontier of Northern Maine, the Craigs and the Sewalls. The firstborn child in this wilderness in 1845 is a sickly boy, my great-grandfather William Windgate Sewall. Despite all his childhood illnesses he survives while many children and childbearing women of that time do not. The cemetery has much evidence. Why does one survive and another dies? Why does one overcome illness and another does not? The mystery of life and death, of nature's call.

Despite the hardships of frontier life, William's mother survives, though she is not young when she has him; his siblings are much older—one brother eighteen years older and one twenty years older. His childhood is spent battling weakness and illness. Diphtheria took many; for him it temporarily took his eyesight. From this experience, he discovers the healing attributes of nature and love. His sister, Sarah, carrying his frail body in her arms, takes him to the riverbed across from their cabin. She reads to him or simply lets him lie there as she paints the beautiful scenery before them, the abounding nature surrounding their log cabin home.

William's childhood is also spent learning from the natives of this land. From the age of three, he learns from the Native American the lessons of the wildflowers, of hunting, of the animals, how to live in and on the bounties of nature. The boy becomes a man, devoted to the parents who nursed him through his sickly childhood. The only thing he prays for is health. In young adulthood, he becomes a strong woodsman, able with logs, whether riding them down a river or felling them in the woods. He becomes a leader of the logging crews, appreciating the natives who work on his crews, unless they are exposed to alcohol, which he feels is good for no man but especially, he observes, ruins the local natives. He lives in a time of prohibition, believes in its law.

It is this great-grandfather's home I inhabit, for who knows how long. Even if for my lifetime, which is unseen, who would want to carry on the legacy after me? We find photos of the family in the library on the third floor, some faces we recognize, many we do not. Daguerreotypes. People long dead. The proclamation from Theodore Roosevelt making my great-grandfather the local tax collector, his lifelong friend, their friendship forged in the same house I inhabit, Sewall House. We find a *Boston Globe* newspaper from 1919 with the headline "Theodore Roosevelt Dies Alone in the Night." There are books written by and about TR on the shelves, fading copies of the letters between from TR to my great-grandfather in a purple cloth binder zipped closed, ink not preserved by being contained, the original letters from Theodore long ago sold at auction. I assume nothing in the home is worth much monetarily: The whale-oil lamp, when appraised, would have been worth more if it had not been turned into the lovely electric lamp now standing in the second-floor landing. The antiques a reminder of the lives lived here, the families raised here, all my relatives, all part of the legacy he said was the house. "This house was built on honor." Will I be able to honor it? How far this feels from my frivolous follies in France. How far it is.

Chapter 3
SOMEDAY

My mother at age three.

"The first step toward success is taken when you refuse to be a captive of the environment in which you first found yourself."

—Mark Caine

At three years old, I prance on the dock, amusing the family in my adorableness as they reach their arms toward me, inviting me to jump in the lake with them, assured that their arms are there to catch, to protect me (how I needed those arms at other times when they were not there). I tip my big toe into the inviting water, then smile and say, "Thumb-day!" further amusing my audience. The truth is, I am terrified. At age seven, when we ride the school bus over to the other Island Falls lake called Pleasant Pond, it is to learn to swim. My Aunt Lib, Uncle Don's wife, who teaches swimming, says she has never seen a child so afraid to put her face in the water. Years later, Aunt Lib marvels that I have jumped out of airplanes and run off to foreign lands.

During my interview with Aunt Nancy for my one-woman show, "This Our Home," thirty years later, Aunt Nancy tells me a story of my mother when she was three, helping me to understand some of the dynamics between me and my mother. When my mother, as photos reveal, was an adorable three, she came prancing down the stairs in her new Sunday dress, much as I pranced on the dock. Filled with pride and joy, her father reprimanded her cruelly for getting joy from the dress that was for church on Sunday, not for dancing with joy and pride. My mother buried her head in Aunt Nancy's lap, the deep shame forming in her young consciousness. My strict grandfather died when I was three; he is barely a memory. Like my brother, my grandfather was legally blind. Unlike my brother, he compensated by achieving, becoming a school superintendent in New Hampshire, my grandmother and her four children—three boys and my mother—moving wherever his job took them. I often wondered what other abuse my mother, the only girl of four children, might have suffered at the hands of her strict father.

When I was seven my mother entered a challenging menopause. She began to suffer from mild depression just as I was struggling with my own developing emotional issues. My mother, other than when her anger rose towards me, was shut down emotionally. We were no help for each other.

My father's childhood fear was his motivator, as it became mine. Born when his mother was nineteen, telling him she wished she had never had him, this not-being-wanted thing we share, loving her son in her own disturbed way. My father's mother had married a man twenty years her senior to escape her own family when she was fifteen. When my father was eleven, his mother moved in with a man across town, leaving my father and his father alone. My grandfather's first wife had been an alcoholic. My grandfather, with concern that he might shame his family again after the alcoholic wife, did not introduce my father to any of his relatives (thus, his grandfather was ninety when he met him) until my father became valedictorian in a high school graduating class of seventeen students in a small New Hampshire town. My father lived in constant fear of something happening to his father, his sole caretaker. Watching the behavior of the men and women at his father's barbershop and pool room, my father realized that climbing out of poverty meant applying his sharp intellect. He did not feel safe until he received his PhD from Columbia at age twenty-six. In June 1941, he married my mother, five years his senior, who had waited five years, letting her know he would also support the mother who had abandoned and not "wanted" him. This was my father—generous, giving, forgiving, ever loving.

"Such a pretty girl."

Chapter 4
MY FAMILY, THE MILLERS

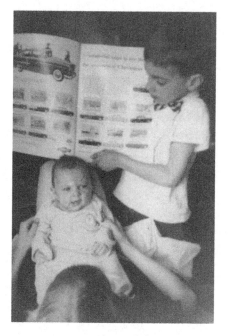

Nancy holding infant Donna, Warren showing us a car book

"Where do I come from? Where did you find me? asks the baby of its mother. She weeps and laughs at the same time, and pressing the infant to her breasts, answers, you were hidden in my heart, darling, you were its desire.

—Rabindranath Tagore

"The way a parent talks to a child
(we talk to our children) becomes their inner voice."

—Peggy O'Mara

Where it all started, a moment of what I can hardly imagine. I never remember them sleeping in the same room, yet I was conceived, the last of four. First was my sister, twelve years older than me, next a boy that died after a few hours, and then my brother, seven years my senior. In the womb, avoiding the outside world as long as I could, I came along to stir things up, delivered three weeks late by Caesarean section. My mother married late by the standards of her time, at age thirty-one (1941), bearing her first child at 33. I was an anomaly for that time, born when my mother was three months shy of forty-five. So unexpected was the pregnancy that when my mother went to the family doctor, complaining that she was not feeling well, he responded by saying, "Mrs. Miller, you have the oldest malady known to womankind. You are pregnant."

Years later, in my thirties, trying to reconcile things with my mother in an effort to band aid our differences, my mother writes me a letter stating that this little girl "came out perfect"—ironic outcome because her chances of having a "perfect" baby were less at almost forty-five. All her other children had been born with some condition: my sister born cross-eyed, my brother with celiac disease at birth and legally blind by age three, and the little guy with inadequate lungs who died within hours. (When asked if he wanted to see the child they lost, my father said no, his tenderness tested by the offering, my caring father not able to bear the viewing of his dead infant.)

Ironically, I arrived in physical perfection and health, a whopping healthy round faced nine pounds eight ounces. As I grew pretty and passionate, my mother made every effort to emphasize developing inner character rather than counting on external gifts, a worthwhile goal pursued in a cutting manner. Her approach resulted in the development of such low self-esteem that I avoided mirrors as I reached my teens, no longer having fun playing pretend toothpaste commercials in the mirror as I had as a youngster. Feelings of inadequacy and imperfection were gradually becoming embedded in me.

My father's father, kind Bumpa (our nickname) Miller, lived with us toward the end of his life, until his psychotic dementia necessitated institutionalization. In our childhood, we would visit my father's mother, long divorced from Bumpa Miller, in her cluttered Concord, New Hampshire, apartment, where she hoarded newspapers and on-sale cases of rubbing alcohol. She signed her birthday cards to us with "Loads of Love," but she didn't seem full of love when she criticized my father every time we went to visit her, accusing him of drinking because his nose was red. The red nose was actually from his respite weekends of sunning in the backyard while he did paperwork.

My brother Warren and I, who have always been close, joked and snickered in the backseat of the car on those visits. Later, as I watched my brother's world unravel into mental illness, hospitalizations, and an inability to function in the outside world, I saw my own developing neurosis magnified in him. He did not act out, as I would, but remained living inside his anxiety, depression, and sadness.

My mother was a good, kind (albeit not warm) intelligent woman. I am not sure we liked each other. I assume we loved each other. She was the strong silent type, I emotional, wearing my heart on my sleeve. We were like fire and water.

One day, as I ran around our neighborhood in Connecticut when I was nine, a barefoot, scruffy-looking tomboy, a neighbor on the hill nearby stopped me long enough to sketch a charcoal of me and write on it, "Such a pretty girl." My mother kept this framed in her attic getaway where she had her bed, her books, her clothes, things that were just hers. (The fact that she kept this sketch all her life meant something, though I was never sure what.) The attic may have been the closest she could get to living as simply as she wished, as she did at the cabin in Maine in the summer, a trait I inherited. (motto for Sewall House "Simplicity in a Complex World").

The attic wasn't terrible. After all, it was my mother's hideaway. She made the space hers, with a full-sized bed by the window, some clothes in the open closet opposite it on one end of the room, and books, family memorabilia, and photos on the other end, including the "Such a pretty girl" sketch. My mother, as mentioned, did not sleep in the same bed as my father. This was her bedroom. In the mind of a child, I did not think of the implications of my mother's private space being a place where she did not share a bed with my father. When I felt lonely, I would ask if I could sleep with her there.

On certain days, however, her hideaway became a dungeon to me. When she locked the door and I was behind it, there was no comfort. Her form of discipline, of punishment, frightened me, making me feel enclosed, helpless, unable to escape. Crying with fear, I kicked and screamed at the door until she decided to let me out. I reflect now on a mother who had a child she had not expected, a woman experiencing a difficult menopause. Although I was statistically the most likely to have had a physical defect, yet being the only child she bore that was physically complete, I would develop a handicap that would take years to overcome. Behind that locked door, my spirit was being crushed.

While the attic she locked me in may have been my mother's Connecticut haven, her Maine cabin on the lake was the real one. My mother took us to Maine as soon as school got out, returning to our home on the hill in Stamford, Connecticut (the little portion called Springdale), just in time to get us back to school. It was on Lake Mattawamkeag that she was content, living a more secluded life than Henry David Thoreau on Walden Pond. Amidst the calm and quiet, the sounds of birds and wind in the trees, the waves lapping at the shore, being in the little log cabin built by her cousin Sam and his father (our Uncle Merrill) with their own hands, was my mother's paradise. These relatives had cut the logs from trees nearby, laid the logs themselves, a beautiful stone fireplace molded for this secluded haven on the shores of the seven-mile-long lake. My mother worked in her teens with her grandparents in their guest cabins a quarter mile away, the place where my grandmother had gone to recover after the rough birth of her first child, my mother. At her cabin, my mother could escape the pace of the cities that stimulated my father, although she quietly tolerated and engaged in community there, accepting the destiny of her marriage to a good man. They were so different in this way—he the extrovert, she the introvert.

I wondered if she had always been so quiet. Years after her death, at Sewall House I found flirty-looking pictures of my mother in her youth, where nothing was discarded. She was a teen, with a boy, a long-lost first crush perhaps. I found provocative posed photos of my grandmother in her youth, fully and modestly clothed but seductive nonetheless, stuck in the Bible by her bed. These photos certainly contradicted my images of the women who had disapproved of me so often and easily in my own childhood. Had they been concerned that I possessed the same precocious streak they had extinguished (or justified, as my grandmother must have, when she married a teacher from the high school she was a student at) in themselves?

Chapter 5
EVERY SUMMER

Every summer, as soon as school got out, my mother packed up our used car for the trip to the cabin. (My brother can recall each car we had in great detail, as well as any outboard motors we had— Asperger's, never diagnosed, is my theory.) The last portion of the journey was Route 2, rolling hills with magnificent forests, occasional tiny towns. The trip north was a full day's undertaking after stopping the night in Warner, New Hampshire, taking a needed break and having a visit at my grandmother's house. In the house in Warner a grandmother (appropriate!) clock in the living room (too small to be a grandfather clock) chimed lightly every hour on the hour. I have a clear memory of sitting on the porch eating watermelon with my Grandmother showing me how to squeeze the seeds between my fingers to make them shoot out like a small stone from a slingshot. This seemed uncustomary behavior for my always so proper grandmother. When I once broke a crystal glass while washing dishes there, my mother getting terrifyingly angry with me, filling me with shame—a vivid imprint; memory of my grandmother coming up to the room I was staying in, reprimanding me harshly, asking why I was so cruel to my mother. She seemed irrational, the experience feeling just the opposite to me.

I loved to run barefoot around the neighborhood in Stamford, Connecticut, where we were during the school year, climbing trees and playing kickball in the yard, our little suburb feeling distant from the city we are a part of. Arriving in Island Falls after the school year in Connecticut, I got to truly experience the immersion of being in the country. Island Falls, the tiny Maine town of a thousand people, houses a clothing store, the Fashion, where my mother purchases our undergarments for return to school; a grocery store that sells cream-filled crusty wonders; and a hardware store where my mother's cousin Sam (one of the three men to inherit Sewall House), who had built her cabin with his father, works happily and helpfully for minimum wage. There is a restaurant aptly called Walt's, the owner's name, in the middle of town with a walk-up window where you can purchase hot dogs and root beer. One hot summer day after wolfing down these items, I proceeded to lose them immediately right on the street.

The ultimate end of the journey every summer is the cabin, five miles down the lake by small aluminum fishing boat, surrounded by water and woods.

Before loading our little boat, we make the rounds to the relatives. The first stop is Aunt Nancy and Uncle Maurice's home (the one now called the Sewall House), looming three stories high as you enter town, placed on top of a little hill to help assuage the effects of runoff from the heavy winter snows. The house still has one of its two original large barns. The bank and post office now take up the space where the second barn had stood, the sprawling Sewall property sold off piece by piece by Aunt Nancy's husband Uncle Maurice to further serve the growth of the town (and his pocketbook).

The town of Island Falls had sprouted up around the homes of the Sewalls and the Craigs, the two founding families. A painting of the first log Sewall home (1845) hangs near the fireplace in the living room at Aunt Nancy's. Uncle Don has one, too. The location of the first house built by the Sewalls, a simple one-room log home, is down the street from Aunt Nancy, on a spot overlooking the river, facing the island and the "falls," nature's gift to viewer and listener. The water always rushed violently after the spring thaw, when it could be heard from Aunt Nancy's wraparound porch. The sound would have been a constant serenade in spring when my great-great-grandparents Levi and Rebecca settled directly across from the falls, (just a spell down from where Aunt Nancy's house is now) the spring water gradually subsiding every summer as the rushing water quieted. This is where my great-grandfather was born in 1845 and where I first arrived in 1955 at age six months.

We follow the annual routine: After visiting Aunt Nancy's white clapboard house in the middle of town, we go to see my mother's cousin Sam and his wife, Audrey, but only if Sam is not working at the hardware store. Then a quick visit to Cleo and Bill, my mother's other cousin, (Bill has the same large strong hands of his grandfather

William Sewall, Bill is said to be the strongest man in the county) and last, but never least, my mother's brother, Uncle Don. (I was called DoDo before birth, as I would be named either Donald or Donna, depending on my sex.) Uncle Don is the local agriculture teacher who uses the plentiful acreage of his peaceful old red farmhouse just outside of town for a pea farm. He and his wife Aunt Lib always have a dog. Like my mother, Uncle Don is a reserved person. He keeps a daily journal of the weather while communing with partridge, deer, and the occasional moose that appear in the fields outside his picture window.

We arrive by boat at the cabin, unpack the bedding and quilts that my mother had stored in metal garbage cans and in my playpen (with screening on top to keep the varmints out) then clean the cupboards, which have been visited by mice (the reason food is kept in cans). Sleeping bags are spread out on canvas army cots against the wall under the windows that gaze out on deep forest, the propane-piped in from a huge container hanging on the back of the cabin- is turned on for the fridge and stove (three solid iron burners set on a countertop). Kerosene lamps are filled to make sure they will give light for reading before sleep. The loons serenade us by night, the other birds in the morning, and, if there is wind at all, the rustling of the leaves. All break the utter silence.

Days are filled with swimming in the tannin-colored water, the color of tea, the water color stained by the leaves and debris brought in by the river. I love playing on the rocky shore with my imaginary friends, with things of nature like the fallen tree that we call the "apartment tree." There are daily tasks, performed mostly by my mother, hand-washing and hanging clothes and bushwhacking and clearing brush to groom the rough, non-landscaped lot. My mother's cousin Sam and his father, Merrill, cut down trees when needed that obstructed the view to Hook Point, the site of the eight self-sufficient Sewall camps. Nature had created an abrupt high slope at Hook Point, a breathtaking spot where my great-grandfather had built eight cabins in the early 1900s, just as Sam and his father had felled the trees nearby to build my mother's cabin soon after World War II. Each cabin at Hook Point had its own porch overlooking the lake. Inside each one-room cabin were two full-sized wood-framed beds, a sink, a small stove, a kitchen table, and several kerosene lamps. Compared to these

camps, my mother's rustic two-story cabin was luxury. On still evenings, we might hear echoes of children's laughter or an adult voice
calling the children from the Hook Point camps, the voices carrying
miraculously more when the air was not moving.

Uncle Merrill, one of my great-grandparents' two sons, and his wife,
Myrtle—nickname Myrkie—ran the camps during the years of my
youth. Aunt Myrkie, with her jovial disposition, made donuts and ice
cream and made sure all tasks were managed to run the place smoothly
for the families who returned to rent the cabins each summer.

In the back was a hunter's shack, very dark inside, where Merrill's
brother Fred lived after his wife died. Uncle Fred was a calm presence with huge strong hands, which had been a legendary part of my
great-grandfather's physique and of Fred's son Bill's as well. My
brother Warren and I loved visiting Uncle Fred in his dark cabin behind the others that faced the shore. Uncle Fred wore heavy work
pants, long-sleeved, button-down plaid flannel work shirts, and heavy
work shoes, even in summer. He had chosen to work in nature as a
potato farmer, a career that had not borne financial fruit. Uncle
Fred's wealth lay in his knowledge of nature's rhythms; he had been
well trained by his father. My great-grandfather had hoped Fred
would further his education but, like other Aroostook County natives
who appreciated the quality of life in northern Maine's nature, he had
no desire to work anywhere but in Island Falls. Uncle Fred would
stand by the shore, look at the sky, then predict the weather for the
next day. He was accepting of all facets of nature, including death. At
age eight, realizing with terror that I was mortal, I remember asking
Uncle Fred if he feared death. "No," he calmly replied, though from
his father he had learned the value of life.

On a day that a dead loon, the graceful black-and-white bird that
dives, glides, and calls upon the lake and is not used for meat or any
other purpose, floated ashore, my great-grandfather admonished
Fred so strongly about the value of life that he would never shoot an
animal unless it was for food. In the same way Native Americans
valued all life, the lesson my great grandfather had learned from them
was imparted and instilled in Fred. Not only human but also animals'
lives were valued. Life was not to be taken away frivolously but with
gratitude, only when needed to keep your own life sustained, a sentiment that would grow in me, as well.

Summers at the lake exposed us to, and imposed on us, lessons of simplicity and mindful consumerism. In Connecticut, my parents were careful to switch off lights, pull down curtains to keep in heat or coolness, not spend on new cars and clothes, thus instilling the New England frugal Puritan ethic in me and my siblings. As Uncle Fred had been taught the value of a life, my New England parents taught us the discipline and mindfulness of minimal spending while my mother shared with us each summer the wealth of nature.

On rainy days, we could watch the clouds turn gray and the wind come up. Great shows of lightning and thunder served as our stage. When I was thirty-three, visiting my parents at the cabin with my boyfriend, a businessman thirteen years my senior who helped draw me from the clutches of promiscuity I had fallen into after leaving my first marriage, a tree ignited just feet from the cabin. This is the only time I saw tears in my mother's eyes. Tears of fear. Within moments, rain came drenching down, exterminating the flame that had sprung up so quickly and so near, its short dramatic dance over.

At age nine or ten while playing alone on the rocky shore as I often did as a youngster, making the big flat rocks into homes for my Barbie and Ken dolls, I saw what looked a big black cat, a lynx I think, appear from nowhere, then disappear the same. I remember no movement, a vision come and gone, forever embedded, however faintly, on my mind, almost as if it did not happen.

There were many happy moments in nature—like cooking hot dogs (before my adult vegetarian days) over an open fire in a little rock fireplace my mother had built outside. We roasted marshmallows at night in the fireplace inside the cabin, ate fresh molasses cookies my mother baked in the metal box that served as an oven when propped up over the propane flames, three burners connected by an iron frame. Campbell's soup—especially tomato—grilled cheese sandwiches, fresh white perch caught by Sam or some other generous fisherman.

From these summer experiences and people grew a deep love for nature and for the gift from my mother: experiencing one of the most beautiful places on earth. Lake Mattawamkeag ran seven miles long and four miles wide, with a natural thoroughfare that led from the wide-open upper lake to the lower lake where our cabin was, as well as a big uninhabited island we could see from our shore. Big

Island sat next to another pristine island of eagles and Norway spruce that was named Norway Island. A site at the end of the lake, on the river that fed it, became a designated State site called Bible Point. Beside the river at the end of the lake was the spot where TR had trekked to read his Bible during his stays with my great-grandparents. Today many go there by ATV (all terrain vehicle). We go by boat and walk in using the pleasant wood trail, as I had as a child, to this tranquil spot with moss cushioning to sit on amidst the smell of pine needles. We sit on the comforting shore with huge tree roots jutting out over the river, meditating where young TR had done the same in his first authentic memorable healing experience in the natural beauty of Northern Maine.

Years later, long after I purchased Aunt Nancy's Sewall House, I had a vivid dream of arriving at the cabin, discovering that two wealthy families had built luxury cabins on either side of our rustic cabin perched on the rocks; ghastly! They had also put in a road. Perhaps a metaphorical premonition of things to come, including a yet unknown upcoming battle to maintain the pristine natural beauty and peace of Lake Mattawamkeag.

Uncle Fred and me on the lake.

Chapter 6
REACHING BACK

Reaching back into my childhood, so many memories, so many no longer vivid. I do not have the amazing memory of my brother, he so handicapped in many other ways. As the red paint peels on Sewall House's sagging porch today, the layers of my memory seem to begin to peel away too, not to reveal *all* of what is under, like the artistic smattering of aged wood that appears under the worn red paint.

Most of my neighborhood playmates in Connecticut during the school year were boys—Jim, Jay, Robbie, the latter who put on musical plays with me in the basement. I remember another neighborhood boy, also named Robbie, walking home from school the day JFK was murdered, saying the murderer should be dragged behind horses. I was nine years old. Later, this Robbie went on to become a Hells Angel, so different from the dancing, singing Robbie who put on plays with me in the basement. The youngest brother of future Hell's Angel Robbie, towheaded Chris, once said to my dad, after Dad told him he had just had a nap and felt like a new man, "You mean you feel like God just made you, Mr. Miller?" Boys—my neighborhood was full of them, and my life would become full of them later, too.

Running around a suburban neighborhood, barefoot whenever I could, climbing the ancient apple tree across the street, which had a small bunch of grape vines behind it, gave me pure delight. By the time I was twelve, a house had been built where the old apple tree had been, occupied by our new neighbors, the Beans, who had one son. I was elated to get the go-ahead the day they asked me to go somewhere with them. I sprinted across the street to their house without looking. The Beans reprimanded me. It could have been the end of my short life. Prone to spurts of joy—or what some might call impulsive acts—this lack of impulse control would lead later in life to destructive behaviors.

A few years before this incident, at age nine or ten, one of the neighborhood boys encouraged me to steal strings of black licorice from Bongo's, a variety store at the bottom of the hill in Springdale, the little Connecticut hamlet where I was raised. I managed to stick the package into my underwear. This act of stealing would go on my list of "sins to heal," the language of a child whose unknown great-grandfather on her mother's side had trickled his Baptist minister lesson of shame through the generations, the beginnings of self-awareness, at attempts to improve.

Another impulse that I began to lose control of was the comfort and joy of eating. I had a ravenous appetite as I matured, could eat multitudinous English muffins in one sitting as I grew into adolescence. During summer visits with my sister in California, her cooking was so good, I would eat until I was stuffed, then laughingly excuse myself to brush my teeth to assuage the over-full feeling. When I began to develop acne, I covered it with layers of unhealthy makeup. Shame was growing inside and erupting on my face—shame for the things I had done but knew I shouldn't have, shame for stifled feelings that became even stronger in adolescence, screaming hormones caused my once smooth skin to add the bumps and crevices of acne to my face's landscape.

This embarrassing outward appearance led to the brilliant idea that if I squeezed the fat out of food, perhaps the grease would not go to my face. Paper towels became my tool, squeezing out hot dogs and hamburgers, only to discover that the after-school donuts from Dunkin', which I categorized as bread, had ghastly amounts of oil in them. Thus began my interest in food and how it affects one's health and looks. Years later, living in Europe, these welts would further their journey along the map of my body, going onto my chest. (Could it be at that time because I broke someone's heart in that chest and was still armoring my own?) This interest in food led to the emotional breakdown of anorexia.

Playing high school basketball with an odd schedule that had no lunch break, the school provided pretzels and grape drinks before practice. These snacks had no grease but also no nutrients. Poor nutrition combined with pushing myself physically in basketball practice, compounded by waiting for the bus sweating from practice as I stood in the winter cold, landed me in the hospital for three weeks with mono. I lost fifteen pounds to jaundice and swollen glands in my groin and armpits, which developed into hepatitis.

When I began to learn more about yoga years later, I discovered in Eastern medicine the liver (the organ of hepatitis) is associated with anger, my rage sublimated, surfacing from the buried layers deep within that morphed into the eating disorder that would develop my senior year in high school, leading me like a phantom into my freshman year of college. When I was fourteen, my brother had made an offhand remark that I was developing a double chin, a teasing jest, probably cause by my increased eating. From his offhand comment, a seed was planted that made me begin to think I was fat. Beneath anger is fear. My fear clutched and dragged me into the deep well of hell that is anorexia. Anxiety neurosis by definition, a subconscious subliminal death wish prevails as you slowly sink into the mire of self-denial and self-loathing anxiety. First comes the denial of feelings, then denial of self in early childhood, feelings of needing to be held, needing to have and express emotions of joy, fear, anger, that were repressed and locked in with the locking of the attic door, which held me behind it with my developing demons. At age twelve, exposure to my brother's fears and demons spiraling down into the nervous breakdown that landed him in an institution only added to my sense that the world was unsafe. My internal questions, unanswered, were rushing at me. No one was there to hold me, to help me understand.

My parents' focus was on Warren and his illness. Drowning in those emotions, I began to deny myself, becoming more and more shut off inside, neither emotionally nourished nor knowing how to fix it, falling deeper into the pit of internal despair.

My escape was spending time with my high school boyfriend and his family, who appeared happy and carefree compared to the achievement-oriented environment of my emotionless home- though in hindsight his mother was a chain smoker and his father obese, masking unresolved things there as well. From time to time, I wrote poems and short stories to sort out my feelings, in hopes of creating a better place in my mind, one of love and less confusion. My mother saved several from the year my brother became ill. Even as a child, I wrote the list of the things I would change (my sins), this process of self-assessment, an effort to improve already beginning. My mother kept this list too, I discovered years later.

Summer visits to my sister in Monterey in my teens, where she now lived for her lawyer husband's job, bleached my hair from the radiant sun and, in the beginning, gave me a sense of freedom. The first summer of freedom, I was fourteen. My sister and her husband Rick were renting a small cottage in Carmel-by-the-Sea. I would walk her husband Rick's bird-hunting pointer dog. The orange-and-white pup would run off the leash down the beach after the seagulls, teasing the birds, it seemed, more than actually pursuing them. I, too, felt "off the leash" with the intimidatingly large waves reminding me that not far from freedom can lie danger—cold, strong, beautiful, and destructive. In contrast, when Rick's native Californian younger brother visited, I marveled at how the dark wild ocean represented a place he could swim joyfully for hours.

I met handsome young military men with fit physiques on the beach who were stationed at the nearby Army base, Fort Ord. My mental scope was limited, not recognizing the contrast of the wealth of this part of California to the military young men often from lesser means. I loved California, a very different beauty and freedom than my isolated yet joyful summers in the Maine woods by the lake.

By the time I was eighteen, those few California weeks were spent in anorexic starvation. My three-year-old nephew Dan, in his developing sensitivity, came up to me with a flower and said, "Aunt Donna, don't be sad." The prospect of adulthood, of leaving my protective, albeit controlling, household instilled a fear that would evolve into the exhilaration of breaking free, that necessary step to finding something or someone (myself) that might or might not ever be found but seemed necessary to search for.

Health had always interested me, particularly exercise, sports, and now nutrition. I entertained the idea of becoming a doctor. My brother-in-law got me a tour of Stanford Medical School with a colleague who was a doctor while I was a freshman at my father's alma mater, the wooded University of New Hampshire. I felt safe in school in those New Hampshire woods, as I had in the Maine woods, but my dream of becoming a doctor was short-lived, cut short by my utter lack of comprehension of calculus.

My mother, who seemed to understand me in some ways while perplexed by me in other ways, would tell me, with no explanation of why, that I was an artist. Perhaps the "art" was life, I thought, the pursuit of mental and emotional health that would come when I discovered Kundalini yoga. After exploring and practicing this yoga for myself, my teacher would urge me within a year of study to pursue the path of sharing it with others. ("You have the aura of a teacher" he said.) Yogi Bhajan said that the biggest saints were the biggest sinners. In my mother's words, "You are going to the devil," I would eventually recognize that the real hell is within ourselves. I believe we have the capacity to turn perceptions around if we look deeply enough, search hard enough, experiment enough with life to discover who we truly are beneath all the voices that have been created within.

■ More Reaching Back:
Slightly Sexual Encounters in Childhood

When my brother Warren was a teen, before his nervous breakdown and downward spiral into a life of mental illness, he was quiet and shy, and from a young age loved cars and boats. (See the photo of Warren showing infant me a car book as my sister holds my arms on page 24.) Legally blind since age three, he would never drive, unlike my also legally blind grandfather, who drove a Model T before the days of testing eyesight. (which led to some car accidents at luckily low speed). Shy Warren did not have many friends. My caring father had said to one of our church friends who taught Warren in junior high "Please take good care of my son. He is a bit different."

Our neighbors had a son Warren's age who often came to watch television with Warren. I loved television so much (escapism or aspiring actress?) that my mother limited the number of hours I watched. Our television was in the basement, which my parents had made into a rumpus room; a small dark attached corner room was the TV room. It was chilly down there, so we had blankets to lay over our laps. This neighbor boy would repeatedly bring me onto his lap, put the blanket over us, then stick his hand under my clothes. I hated when he fondled me, felt no pleasure from it, but never told my mother. I was already, at seven, feeling the protector of the brother I loved who had few friends. I never told anyone about this boy's offenses. Years later, I went to his mother's funeral. The guy I was seeing at the time, Z, told me I must confront him. I was angry with Z for being so controlling but also terrified about confronting this offender from my past, at a funeral no less. In the end, for whatever speculated reason, he did not show up at his own mother's funeral, much to my relief.

The guardian of the patch of ice that we skated on as small children was a handsome older man with silvering hair, a sturdy body, and sharply defined facial features. Our outdoor "skate rink" was a swamp at the bottom of a hill near our home, a beautiful nature spot with a bit of forest, where I caught tiny crayfish in the spring. One day when I was nine, this gentleman offered to give me a ride home. In front of my house (how audacious) as we sat in the car, he French kissed me. I never took a ride with him again.

My mother once left me with an elderly distant cousin to babysit me in Maine when I was five. He fondled me, kissed me, and made out with me. I told my mother, who never left me with him again.

The fourth experience I recall was when I was ten or eleven and the boy was twelve. He was a recent import from England. I don't remember how he came into my life. We also ended up in that family basement, under the ping-pong table, where he exposed a flaccid penis, attempting to have intercourse with me. Failed attempt Thank God.

None of these experiences gave me pleasure, only a feeling that what these men and boys were doing to me was not fun or right. These incidents, though mild compared to incest or full-blown sexual abuse, combined with my developing questions about self-worth, compounded a confusing sense of the secrecy of shame and sexuality.

"Teachers open the door but you must enter by yourself."
—Zen proverb

There was the secret shame of uninvited sexual encounters and there was shame from female adult authority figures. In eighth grade at Dolan Junior High School in my hometown of Stamford, Connecticut, my homeroom English teacher was a teacher whose name oozed her stern demeanor. She dressed her thin frame impeccably, coiffed her flimsy chin-length, wavy dyed-brown hair, and skillfully applied full war paint. Her makeup was not overdone, but it was clear that she took time with it as she did with her well-matched skirts, blouses, and cardigan sweaters. Her teaching of *A Tale of Two Cities* explained the importance of the words, names, and imagery in the book, thus planting the subconscious seed of appreciation for the word written well at the same time another was planted by my mother and grand-mother—the seed of shame. For assignments, I wrote short stories of green-eyed boys like the one I met at summer church camp and poems about the questions of life and nature.

She required us to read "The Adventures of Tom Sawyer" which gave me a love for the writing of Mark Twain. I had found a con-densed version at home and was reading it in homeroom, Fitzy stalk-ing up and down the aisles, pouncing on me like a cat on a mouse when she discovered me reading a condensed version. She dragged me into the hallway. "You think you are a little queenie," she hissed through her teeth behind the red lipstick. I thought fire might next emerge from her nostrils. My eyes held back the hot tears, so trained already not to show emotion, to stifle the shame. The same feelings arose as during the punishment behind closed doors, feelings of be-ing misunderstood, of no one asking for my explanation of why I did things when I felt confused, shocked out of my innocent belief that I was doing nothing wrong. The weeds of shame sprouted a little more in the flowerbeds of my mind.

Years later, when I was in my fifties, I heard that Fitzy was alone in the assisted living facility where my father lived (and would also die). She, to my knowledge, died alone. A cab driver told me, after I said goodbye to my ninety-nine-year-old father en route to catch the train back to New York from the facility one night, "If you have no children you will be alone. No one will take care of you."

Fitzy and I had, after all, had something in common.

Chapter 7
FAMILY PHOTO

"The only true disability is a crushed spirit."
—Aimee Mullin

Fear
Fear passes from man to man
Unknowing,
As one leaf passes its shudder to another
 All at once the whole tree is trembling
and there is no sign of the wind.
—Charles Simic

"First know in self what thou hast believed, and then set that as the ideal... And when the darker days come, and when the shadows come that would make thee afraid, turn within and have a good time at scaring the bogies away from those that would fear, that would doubt."
—Edgar Cayce Reading 815-2

I was afraid to put my face in the water when I learned to swim. However, once I learned, I stayed in the water until my face turned blue. I jumped out of an airplane, discovering a natural high, a literal step parting me momentarily from fear, only to break my back on the second jump. I walked out of a marriage and a career that was idyllic, running to faraway lands, to cultures completely unknown. What was the thing leading me to and through all this? The voice of fear.

If something did not scare me, put me out of my comfort zone, become too comfortable, I rejected it. The need to face the fear seemed to be, whether it was rational or not, the drive to overcome the deep-rooted lack of self-esteem combined with the desire to ignite my spark of human spirit that ached to experience the adventure of life, despite the Fitzies and my mother's and grandmother's voices telling me not to. When I was fifty, finding out from my brother (he who remembers such details from our childhood while I remember so little) about a conversation he overheard between my mother and grandmother saying "What will ever happen to Donna?" when I was only eight years old. Even when a child does not hear these things, they feel them.

The unconscious acting out in my life from the age of twenty-seven to the age forty felt like a reaction to the matriarchs in my family who had spurned me from childhood, exemplified by these comments made when I was an innocent eight-year-old sitting on a stoop licking an ice cream cone. What caused them to make such a comment? What terrible thing was I doing in that moment, or in any of the ones they judged me for? Were they the victims of their own repressions, their experiences (or lack thereof), their lost dreams, their own feelings projected onto me of who they had once had the freedom to become? Was it because of all this that I never wanted children?

These women had reprimanded me, disappointed me, punished me for not doing it "their" way, not encouraging or accepting me. I imagine that these women had their own hidden wounds, deeply stored away. I would never know these wounds, only be the victim of them.

By age twelve, when my brother had his nervous breakdown, in a family photo my head juts forward, cutting it off from my body, cutting myself off from my feelings. By the time I left my first marriage nearly fifteen years later, my body was aching to explore those cut off feelings, with no examples, no tools, no knowledge of how to deal with feelings, only the desire to break out of the repressed mold. The media presents sexiness as a desirable thing, synonymous with love—sex brings attention, sex means approval. With time and experimentation, I discovered it was none of these. For years, the unexpressed feelings erupted into lust. I made a list of my lovers after my modeling years. My list totaled 80, a number that amused me, at the time making me strangely proud. But my experiment finally proved that sex, lust, passion does not equal love.

Addiction was buried under the craving for excitement, numbing the emotional pain that had been so repressed: Addiction feels good, instead of dealing with what is really going on deep inside you. I substituted sex or a substance for facing the feelings. Years in various dramas culminated in years of chasing someone who was passionate, exciting, and controlling, with his own addictive behaviors around pot and women.

Eventually my story became one of transforming the feelings back to the things that had touched me as a child—nature, friends, authentic relationships—no longer from the thrilling touch of a stranger.

I discovered the many ways people and the world can be, the mirrors that reflect the parts of ourselves we want and need to be and do not want to be. I grew to learn that the most important thing was my conscience, my awareness. It would take years of my adult life, years of yoga and meditation, experiences of daring fun and hurt at the same time. Discovering Kundalini yoga would be the catalyst for the shift, finding that the intuitive voice inside knows that one's truth can become more heard. A chance conversation with a woman I met over drinks, when I first returned to the United States from Paris in 1985, changed my life. This woman gave me a tiny slip of paper with Ravi Singh's number. "I think you would like this yoga. I do," she said. Within a week, my lost thirty-year-old self walked into Ravi's Kundalini Yoga class, walking out sensing that this was something that would heal my inner life.

I am the one with my head jutting forward, second from the right front.

"In surrender the head bends and meets the heart. The head that does not bend has no value, and the head that is stiff will have to bend sometime, either in surrender or in shame. The head that bends in surrender will never have to bend in shame. Shame accompanies arrogance. Shyness accompanies love. See how children are endowed with shyness, that is natural. Shyness is inherent. Shame is inflicted by society and is acquired. Shame brings guilt and shyness adds to one's beauty. Retain your shyness and drop your shame."

—Sri Sri Ravi Shankar

Donna and Warren—miss animated/mister buddy.

"The soul is dyed the color of its thoughts. Think only on those things that are in line with your principles and can bear the light of day. The content of your character is your choice. Day by day, what you do is who you become. Your integrity is your destiny—it is the light that guides your way."

—Heraclitus

Chapter 8
WHAT COUNTS?

"What you can endure, you can cure."

—Yoga master Yogi Bhajan

"Yoga teaches us to cure what need not
be endured and endure what cannot be cured."

—Yoga Master Iyengar

"If you encourage your children to stay connected to Source Energy, they will remain clear-minded; they will remain optimistic; they will remain enthusiastic. They will remain balanced; they will remain flexible. They will remain in a state of grace. They will remain in a state of Well-Being. And they will make wonderful choices."

—Abraham Hicks

What counts?

I spent years thinking that being thin was a way to get noticed, when actually I was shrinking myself in my need for the attention my disturbed ego was searching for, anorexia the result of this deep, unresolved disturbance. Through inner fortitude and a new life direction, I managed to gradually conquer a disease that kills some of its victims. I moved on to becoming excessively sexually active, something that, in my insecurity, seemed appropriate in the modeling world. Still mired in low self-esteem, I sought attention and approval in unhealthy behaviors (as Yogi Bhajan said, looking for God in all the wrong places). When I discovered Kundalini yoga, with its "yogi" concept of not reacting to impulses, but rather responding to life, this awareness and practice would become the catalyst that healed my life.

Years after that discovery, now in my fifties, I attended an event with the world-famous Kundalini yoga teacher Gurmukh, whose center I teach at in New York City. A man from India whom she calls a living saint was teaching. The topic was happiness—or specifically, being healthy, happy, and holy, which is also what 3HO stands for (the Kundalini Yoga organization). In the pursuit of happiness, Americans seek material things, yet many are on pills for their day-to-day experience. The premise of the talk was that to be happy means to learn to be content and constant no matter the waves of the ocean of life, which, in turn, means training the mind.

The evening took me back to reflections on anorexia, a deeply emotional disease about control and food, a self-loathing hard to describe. Food is nurturance, as is affection. The woman who spoke for the swami on this evening suggested that if we are held in our mother's arms we feel safe, that we would do anything, including jump into the ocean, if we are in our mother's arms. There is also the divine mother who holds us in her arms. I wondered if this was why I had often felt unsafe in the world, wondering why survival, including money, eats at my conscience with anxiety. The speakers this night spoke of discipline, of how a yogi is disciplined. I now had learned to be disciplined through my yoga practice, with not overspending and living within my means, but still feeling deep down that I had not overcome my obstacles. Do we ever?

After years of living in "careful" poverty, both financially and emotionally, my second husband brings $100,000 in student loans to our marriage in 2004. (debt another way to bring up the feeling of being unsafe). He encourages me to improve Sewall House, paying for the improvements on credit. He adds more debt for his "music studio." I feel I am falling off a cliff. Is this relationship to help me face my fears, to become empowered, taking risks, or to deepen the fear in my life? I was raised, and have actually lived with, an awareness of budget and balance, having an allowance and a checkbook to balance as a child. Neither of my husbands wrote down their checks, as I always have. My first husband had enough money that he did not need to keep track of his finances, in contrast to my second husband, who had no assets (other than his multiple talents) and the assets we built together.

Going back to this, being held by the mother brings a feeling of safety. Fear that you will not have enough, feeling that you are just getting by—does it stem from not being held in the safe arms of a mother so you never feel safe? Anorexia, the cry for attention from mother, who is meant to nourish and support you from day one, to hold you in her arms and make you feel safe; these feelings offer an uphill battle to create that for yourself. I look back on being twelve, when my brother was hospitalized in an institution where James Taylor and Art Carney had also been treated, my parents dutifully driving us to Hartford to see my brother on weekends. I remember the place, the feeling of an institution where people stay within sterile walls. I remember my mother pulling me aside, telling me to be grown up now as we focused on Warren's needs, the same mother who, years later when she welcomed her only great-grandchild, would balk at holding him, saying, "I don't like to hold babies."

I did not know what *grown up* meant, entering the awkward adolescent phase of life. My mother was asking me to be there for my brother. Who would be there for me? My father, my rock, was often working. Panic became a familiar feeling, my mother being physically there, my needs provided for but un-nurtured emotionally. During her difficult menopause (she would later send me articles on menopause as a warning for what she perceived as an impending awful time in life), her own struggles and demons competed with the challenges of Warren's illness. Like my mother's grandmother Mary Sewall, who had been torn away from her family to serve as a housekeeper at age twelve, I too was expected to be "on my own" in a way at an age of challenging transition, still a child but feeling the changes happening within that would bridge the gap into adulthood. My mother had written about the challenges my great-grandmother had faced at age twelve in her self-published story of her grandmother's life, expressing well the feelings of her grandmother at twelve but not recognizing mine.

By the time I was fourteen, the family doctor predicted that I would have psychological issues. He offered to have me come live with him and his wife and daughters, asking me about my sexuality, sensing the emotional repression of my home. My mother thought he was a pervert, though his sensitivity came at a time when I needed someone to see my pain. By the time I finished high school, my five-foot-seven frame had dropped to 90 pounds. What had started as an attempt to avoid greasy foods to dissuade teen acne had developed, insidiously, into a full-fledged eating disorder. My freshman year at the University of New Hampshire, the family doctor who had suggested these underlying issues advised that unless I was able to get to 110 pounds, I would not be able to return to school. I was sent to a school psychologist at the university, a man who told me to sit in the "child's pose" (sitting on your heels, your body folded forward with your forehead on the floor). This was my first exposure to yoga. I thought it was bizarre and stupid. I felt nothing.

Though I was ill, my strong will, the same one that had starved me, was able to get myself up to the required 110 pounds. The non-eating eating rituals took time to change. I had a relapse to 90 pounds at age twenty-four, before my wedding. Like any addiction, anorexia can relapse. I was able to overcome it after the second bout, fighting internally the struggle that can last a lifetime or lead to death.

At eighteen, I felt the distinct impulse to grab a knife from my parent's knife rack on the wall and kill myself, the emotions and self-loathing of anorexia all too complex to understand. ("Either commit suicide or find a way out of your misery."—*Osho*) My fear of death was as strong as the other fears I was battling. The moment passed. The emotional issues, however, did not. Determined not to feel this way forever, I found my own way to search for the arms that did not hold and comfort me, until I realized they are my own.

When I was fourteen that family doctor saw my repressed family, not only sexually, but in the normal day-to-day affection between loved ones. I am forever grateful for that first acknowledgment that the external appearance of "normal" can hide internal dysfunction. I ruminated on this as I heard the living saint's words, as I have many times, still sorting out the reasons for it all in my mind. And if you can endure, you can cure—or at least keep the demons at bay.

Me at 90 pounds.

■ **October 8, 2013, day of this entry:**

By the end of my freshman year at UNH, where I enjoyed the woods that reminded me of Maine, providing clean-aired running terrain, my anorexia slowly becoming healed, I learned another lesson—that the simplicity and intricate beauty of nature that I loved could be cruel.

There was a group of daring earthy students that loved the outdoors, skiing the challenging nongroomed steep hills, climbing nearby mountains. One sparkling warm spring day, they took a dip in a river, one young man taking a shallow dive into waist-deep water. I stood on the bridge with my bicycle, watching as his face stayed head-down in the water, his body unmoving. That impulse of joy brought him complete paralysis when his neck hit a rock under the surface of the water. I had felt the energy of the mental/emotional paralysis I was just beginning to awaken from. I realized the gift to walk, run, stretch, and jump those blocks out of my tissues.

When I was told by my doctor that I could not go back to school unless I brought my skeletal self up to 110 pounds, I realized it was my own emotions that were causing my paralysis of self. I had a choice to put the weight back on, unlike my fellow now-paralyzed student, who accepted his fate with grace. I could move on, jog at night with two grad students, and nurture my newfound dream of becoming a doctor. Though this dream was short-lived, I learned from that moment how quickly things can change, to be grateful for an intact body that could choose paths of motion and life directions, in themselves the gifts of freedom.

"Of the Seven Deadly Sins, anger is possibly the most fun. To lick your wounds, to smack your lips over grievances long past, to roll over your tongue the prospect of bitter confrontations still to come, to savor the last toothsome morsel of both the pain you are given and the pain you are giving back—in so many ways it is a feast fit for a king. The chief drawback is that what you are wolfing down is yourself. The skeleton at the feast is you."

—Frederick Buechner, 1926

My first ever modeling picture, taken in Fresno, California.

Chapter 9
MISUNDERSTOOD

I am

I am a girl who wonders.

I wonder what people think.

I hear gossip.

I see my reflection in the mirror.

I want to be recognized.

I am a girl who wonders.

I pretend to be famous.

I feel people looking down on me.

I touch my heart to see if it isn't broken.

I worry if people talk about me when they seem to like me.

I cry when I am away from people and think what I have done.

I am a girl who wonders.

I understand people who do love me for who I am.

I say, I will be recognized.

I dream that one day people see me for who I am.

I try to be smarter.

I hope that one day I can be me!

I am a girl who wonders.

—Sierra Hodgdon (my informal "adopted daughter"
in Island Falls, Maine, whom I met through
offering a free yoga class for children in 2010).

As I approached graduation from the University of New Hampshire in 1976, I applied to Berkeley and San Diego for my dietetic internship. I wanted to be in California, where I had felt free when visiting my sister during summers in Monterey (and because the family doctor told me to get as far away as possible from my family). Rejected by Berkeley, I was accepted at Mercy Hospital in San Diego, a beach-town paradise that included a Stamford High School buddy who had returned to her hometown. Cindy and I had run track together, been in a social girls' club called Siguaras, and in the close-knit Congregational church youth group where I met my first boyfriend. Cindy lived at the beach. We were both blonde athletic girls in our early twenties ready to move on to the next phase of life. The beach seemed ideal to me, who craved living in nature. I moved in with Cindy, walking distance from the beach, which I decided over the suggestion from the internship director, a matronly woman named Mildred Smith, that we should live near the hospital downtown. My dad bought me an old green convertible Volkswagon Kharmann Ghia with the back chopped off. I could commute the ten minutes to the hospital. I was on my way!

The dietetic interns were a diverse group—Jennifer, from nearby La Jolla, became my best friend. She was cool, warm and laid back, busty and funny. Sister Pat, the nun who was so thin I wondered if she had anorexia or was simply paranoid about her high cholesterol. Wendy, a cute, tiny Asian girl, full of smiles and always fun, also became a friend. She was so tiny she could ride on the back of my new California boyfriend Ron's Goldwing motorcycle with me. The few other interns have faded from my memory. Jennifer stayed a good friend for years, Jennifer, who reached out to console me on the distraught day that Mildred "called me into her office."

I hadn't done anything wrong: I was punctual, as I am to this day (I had a time-urgent father, trained well by his conscientious example); my well done assignments were handed in on time. Mildred's issue was that I did not fit the "dietitian" mold. I wore no makeup, didn't wear a bra. I wore a slip (our uniform was much like the white nurse-type dress of the day), which I assumed covered enough. My intention was not to be rebellious. Mildred, stern and proper like my mother, was uptight and scary to me, another symbol of the woman whose approval I would never get.

Mildred called me in, accusing me of being a party girl. The feelings of disapproval and shame stung me, as unjustified as saying that I was going to the devil or that no man would ever love me. It was like déjà vu to that time in eighth grade when the teacher had called me Queenie. Other than wanting to mold me, Mildred did not have any grounds for the accusations. My small breasts didn't need a bra, I thought. I was a responsible, good student and intern, unconscious of the importance of superficial image, which meant nothing to me as it did to the world of rules.

I was devastated. Jennifer tried to console me with a hug, but I was unable to accept her affection. Pushing her away, I did not know how to accept something no one had offered me as a child. Here I was at twenty-two with no understanding of the comfort of affection or how to respond to it. My mother's brother, Uncle Don, my name-sake, once stated it clearly: "The Harmons (my mother's maiden name) don't hug." The women in my family kissed each other on the lips as my mother quickly did on her mother's and Aunt Nancy's mouths, my confusion compounded by this weird little expression of love between but no hugs or comforting touch.

Someone was about to come into my life who made no judgment of me, who truly loved and accepted me just as I was. My roommate Cindy introduced me to Ron, a handsome, fun-loving guy raised in La Jolla, the same town Jennifer was from. Cindy had told me about her boyfriend Kevin's skydiving buddy Ron, how adorable and nice he was. When some forgotten person's wedding came up, I got to meet Ron. I was his date. We had fun sex that night which felt natural. He didn't rush to call me afterwards, nor did I wait for his call. Three weeks later, he called to see if I wanted to go waterskiing— which I had never done so he taught me—Ron, the talented athlete who could waterski barefoot and do tricks on waterskis. A boy who'd grown up near the beach of La Jolla, Ron was working as a lifeguard on the San Diego beaches. His first gift to me was a full wetsuit. It was easy to be with him, to do things with him. For once, I didn't feel self-conscious. I could hardly believe such a great guy was falling for me so quickly, but it felt so right.

Within months, I moved into his apartment near the San Diego beach where he worked. Ron would later prove how amazing he was when he nursed me during my recovery from my skydiving accident.

After my back healed, we moved to five raw acres that Ron's mother gave us in the exclusive town of Rancho Santa Fe, north of San Diego, living in a trailer during mud season as we designed and built a small house at the end of a road overlooking a canyon. I ran a marathon a year after breaking my back to prove to myself that my body still was of service to me and my active lifestyle in sunny Southern California, which I had grown to love with my new life and new friends and most of all, with Ron.

To build his flight hours for his new interest, Ron took a job in the Mojave Desert, flying radioactive materials and explosives for the government. I took on the responsibility of preparing our wedding, which was to be held in the backyard of our newly constructed home. Commuting the two hours each way to Riverside to get my master's in nutrition at the Seventh Day Adventist University Loma Linda, I did research on cholesterol, I relapsed into anorexia, back down to 90 pounds a second time. The pressures of getting our home built, of living in a trailer, of commuting to school for my master's degree, mixed with the subconscious stress of the responsibilities of my upcoming marriage, took their toll on my reawakened demons and the fears of adulthood that triggered the deep anxiety of anorexia.

Despite having shrunk to ninety pounds for a second time, on June 19, 1979, staring into Ron's blue eyes, I sang Peter Paul and Mary's wedding song. After the wedding, my 90-pound self began once again to gain weight, more importantly I began to heal. Modeling photos (my new interest) from that time show me toothpick thin. Despite the Connecticut doctor's not being there to tell me what weight I had to get back up to, I managed to gradually get there myself. Anorexia is a self-obsessed illness I am grateful that I had the strength to survive. Life appeared good. With Ron I felt understood, loved, and accepted. When he was relocated to Fresno to build his flying career, I myself chose to fly—on to other adventures, still mired in yet another layer of emotional demons.

Ron got an opportunity to fly for a rancher in Fresno, the company called Harris Farms. We had a small house on the huge acreage where the ranch raised cattle and oranges. I missed the little house we had designed in Rancho Santa Fe, missed our life in San Diego with Ron's friends and mine, but the move made sense for our careers so I did it without question. Here in inland California, we made fresh-squeezed juice from the most delicious big oranges I have ever tasted, grown on the farm where we now lived.

Soon Ron began to also fly for a family that owned a vineyard. One of the owners, I heard, had mentioned that Ron Davidge's wife was a "K.O." I had no idea what that meant.

The modeling seed was planted in Fresno when I was running a nutrition program for an Indian (Native American) health project. A young woman who came to the clinic asked if I would model my legs for a local ad campaign. I put on a man's jacket, faced the wall with my elbows bent and fingers spread wide on the wall, turned back to look at the camera for my first modeling photo. At the time, I was part of a private dietetic practice that worked with doctors, which resulted in my becoming the nutrition spokesperson for a local talk show as well as being published in nutrition publications. Though my nutrition career was blossoming, the modeling job sparked something a few people had suggested, encouraged me to do in my younger years.

One of my clinic coworkers, a Hispanic man who worked in my department as a nutrition counselor claimed to be psychic, said that he could see it. I asked him what he saw. He said that unless it was positive, he would not tell the person. I persuaded him. He told me that within a year my marriage would be over.

Ron was now also flying in Fresno for a wealthy local businessman. The man had two Jaguars; he said you needed two because they are such temperamental cars that one was always at the shop. Ron and I often met for lunch. We were a close couple, doing extremely well professionally. Things worked easily between us. I was able to purchase expensive clothes for my life as a businesswoman. We moved into a house in a cul de sac with three bedrooms and a kidney-shaped pool that we rarely used. I began driving the Porsche back and forth from Fresno to San Francisco as I weaned myself away from the nutrition field, moving toward modeling and away from Ron, away from our idyllic marriage. I had found nurturance in creating our first house. Being torn from it had triggered something deep inside. It felt like we/I had rejected the home of my marriage. I missed my friends in San Diego, but otherwise I thought Ron and I were okay. (Ron told me fifteen years later, when I met him for dinner during a layover in New York City for his job with American Airlines, that I had been selfish. I had not seen my work colleague's prediction unfolding, had been very upset with him when he told me, sure that he was wrong.)

An eye doctor at the clinic I worked at, an Asian woman, convinced me to take EST (Erhard Seminar Training), the then popular course for self-evolution presented over a few weekends. Taking this course would be the catalyst for me to burst out.

Werner Erhardt started the EST movement, with its own language ("I got it") and quick-fix weekends where you could not leave the room, even to pee, until they let you. It later became the more lenient Forum, with the same practice of lecture, share, and process behind closed doors with a huge audience led by one trainer. I had my first affair with a participant, then with a trainer. It was EST that gave me the "courage," as I saw it at the time, to leave nutrition for modeling.

I was falling into the abyss of sabotaging the good life prescribed by society. I lacked the sense of self required for an authentically fulfilling life. I told Ron about the first affair, which happened when he was off flying; he cried and forgave me, no anger, only hurt loving sadness. I continued to do it—with my EST trainer, with men I would meet modeling or at a bar in San Francisco. Neither Ron nor I had the emotional equipment to know that this was a cry from something deep within me that could not be fixed quickly.

My restless self kept moving, on to San Francisco. I joined a modeling agency run by a gay man named Jimmy Grimme, who told me I had the ugliest feet he had ever seen, bony with bunions that had started to develop in high school and would get larger with each year. He thought the rest of me was good enough for his agency. When a modeling agency from Paris put me on a wait list, I decided to go to Europe for three months, having been assured by photographers that I had tested (shot photos) well, and that if I went for three months, I would get tear sheets (pictures in magazines) which would prepare me to get paid work in the States. After a year in Europe, Ron sent me divorce papers. He was brokenhearted, got into cocaine for a short while, totaled his Porsche driving into the back of a truck he did not see in the morning fog of Fresno, requiring facial surgery as a result. Part of me felt badly, but my other parts were pulling me forward into the insanity of the modeling pursuit. I would not return to the States for three years, continuing to act on impulse toward destructive behaviors.

In 1985, Kundalini yoga would enter my life. This yoga taught me how to replace the demon-driven habits with constructive habits, physically and emotionally. Through years of fluctuating through lightness and darkness, healthier habits prevailed. Kundalini yoga made me realize that what I was doing was not filling the void; it was hurting me and others. My experimentation had been a reaction to repressed feelings in childhood. I discovered that what I wanted was the joy of my innocent friendships from childhood, the friends who now write me about how warm and wholesome I had been, the young woman Ron had fallen in love with, the true self Kundalini yoga taught about. My accomplished friend Tony, a photographer in Europe, told me I had a good heart, but that "someone had done a number on it." My own feelings of isolation and fear began to shut my heart down, buried in anxiety. Kundalini yoga awakened the pure feelings of joy I'd once had, before the contaminated conditioning of shame spiraled me away from the healthy choices, the simple moments of pleasure. The Kundalini Yoga Master Yogi Bhajan taught that happiness is our birthright. I was determined to find it, just as I had been determined to leave the comfort of marriage, love, acceptance, and a career, which had not led me to it.

"Bunion: analogous to the knots of life.
Lack of joy in meeting the experiences of life.
Affirmation: I joyfully run forward to greet life's
wonderful experiences."

—Louise L. Hay in *Heal Your Body*

Chapter 10
BROKEN BACK, BROKEN SELF

When I was twenty-two, life was good. I graduated from my dietetic internship in San Diego right after graduating college in 1976, which led to a fun job at a federally funded program called Preventative Medicine through Nutrition. I traveled to eleven community clinics in San Diego counseling different ethnic groups from Filipinos to Mexicans (in my broken Spanish) on healthy eating choices. My boss was a laid-back beach bum who showed up for work in shorts and loose, open shirts, bearded and probably handsome though his Santa Claus belly belied the overall look, pipe hanging from his mouth, bare feet thrown up on his desk. Little did I realize that this veering away from a standard dietetics job was the beginning of my awakening unconventionality.

Ron and I were living together in his apartment a few blocks from the beach, a fact I kept from my parents. His pet piranha Brutus was the conversation piece of our living room. When he cleaned the fish tank, I would step up on a chair until he was done, frightened that the flesh-eater would jump out of the pail and take a piece of me. We rode down to Rosarita beach in Mexico on weekends on the same motorcycle we would later take on our honeymoon, a big Honda Goldwing, accompanied by his friend Larry, who resembled Tom Selleck. We feasted on lobster omelets and fresh tortillas with super-strong hot sauce, the real thing, for two dollars. Ron was raised a vegetarian—a pescatarian, actually, as I had recently chosen to be—by his animal-loving, extremely animal-zealous, Christian Scientist mother. With schooling behind me, as well as my emotional issues (so I thought), I was experiencing a firm fun foot on life.

We had potluck parties with friends. His friends became mine, my friends became his.

An activity Ron loved was skydiving. His good friend Kevin was dating my best friend and roommate Cindy. Cindy and I often went to watch the boys skydive on weekends.

One weekend, I suggested to Cindy that we take the one-day skydive training course to give it a shot ourselves. Ron was hesitant about my trying to skydive—one prior girlfriend had sprained and one had broken an ankle trying skydiving. I brushed his warning off. It was 1977. I was twenty-two. The first jump would be made after the day of training, which taught you how to jump and what to do if things went wrong—pull the reserve chute— how to step out onto the stick connected to the small airplane, arch your back, then let go, the most frightening moment, the metaphorical one of *letting go*. On a static line, the parachute opens after a few seconds of free fall. Free fall could reach 120 mph in the stable belly-down position you hoped to attain by arching your back before stepping off the "stick."

It was a California desert day, hot and dry. The required full uniforms made it even hotter. The jump went off without a glitch. Stepping out onto the strut is the most terrifying moment. Falling quickly on static line, alone in the air, until the chute opens, you barely have time for thought. The feeling after the chute opened was the most euphoric experience I'd ever had, floating toward earth in utter silence after the exhilarating moment of speed before the chute opened, giving a slight jolt upward before floating for a few minutes back to solid ground. The whole week after my first jump, I felt as if I had conquered death, or at least a good deal of my fear.

The false euphoria of conquering death (after all, who does?) would kick me in the butt, literally. The following week, I could not wait to skydive again. This time, the same euphoria, the same serenity as I floated toward the earth, until I hit the ground. The chutes in the 1970s were not as aerodynamically foolproof as they are today, nor did you go tandem with an instructor. The force of landing can be very strong if you are downwind, which I was. Unlike my perfect landing the week before, my landing this time was hard, my instinct for a parachute landing fall, called PLF (falling to your side, first to the hip, then the shoulder), not yet developed. Had I not fallen back onto my coccyx, had I done a PLF, it might have been strong but different. Instead, my whole spine took the impact of the landing. A searing pain went up my back. I could not move or get up. Ron ran out onto the field. I was rushed to the hospital. In the emergency room, he—one of the most laid-back people I knew—screamed at the nurse when she went to move me, knowing that whatever was going on could be worsened by moving me until they knew what it was. Ron's years as a lifeguard on the beaches of San Diego had trained him well for spinal injuries, people surfing and body surfing, sometimes paralyzed by injuries to the spine.

The diagnosis, when it came, was a compression fracture to T-12. Years later, through yoga, I would find out this is a fragile vulnerable part of the spine, important for bending back. That day, all I knew was that I was put in a hospital bed, calling my parents to tell them that I had jumped out of an airplane, had broken my back, but hardest of all was telling them I was living with Ron, living in sin.

Fueled by my stubborn independent nature, juxtaposed to fear, I stayed in the hospital only three days. There was talk of surgery; I insisted no. The doctor said if I could sit up within three days, I could go home—otherwise, surgery. I sat up, much to his surprise and much to my agony.

Without knowledge or research, for whatever reason, my intuition told me surgery was an option that would only lead to more pain, a small intuitive voice rising to test the voices of authoritative convention.

I went home and lay flat on my back for a month. Cindy knew a chiropractor who had experienced the exact same vertebral fracture in a car accident. He suggested I put a board under my mattress, not move for a month, just let my body heal itself. At that time, Ron was learning to fly, dutifully returning home during the day between flying lessons to help with my bedpans. (Years later, after we had divorced, Ron became a pilot for American Airlines, where my mother's youngest brother Uncle Windy, an appropriate nickname for his given name Windgate, apt name for a pilot, no? and the middle name of my great grandfather, had been a top-ten senior pilot before retiring,)

After a month of lying flat on my back, not easy for high-energy me who preferred to sleep on my side or stomach, the chiropractor gave me a corset so that I could begin to walk. My mother came from Connecticut to help, with more disapproval, I am sure, realizing that I was living with a man outside marriage. In her strong silent demeanor, the pressing thing at the moment however was supporting my recovery—a good woman, a dutiful mother, a repressed, emotionally shut-down person who knew not how to comfort. I was uncomfortable around my mother, even afraid of her who had locked my unruly self in the attic with her cruel prophesies for me, yet still craved her love, attention, and approval.

After three months of walking, I was allowed to sit. The first shower I took, I passed out, my body so weak and atrophied. Once again, Ron was there. He passed the door to the bathroom, catching me before I fell.

I vowed to get back to my athletic self. Within a year I ran that San Diego marathon, having run track in high school and college (though the high school record I broke for the 880 was broken again the next year). Years later, in 1985 I would run a half marathon in Paris before returning to the States after three years, both races marking turning points in my life.

Chapter 11
M̧ILL V̧ALLEY, 1982

"I don't fear failure—
I fear succeeding at something that doesn't matter."

—Dan Grickson

❧❧❧❧❧ ❧❧❧❧❧

"There is only one success—to be able to spend your life in your
own way."

—Christopher Morley

❧❧❧❧❧ ❧❧❧❧❧

"My suggestion is that whenever you have to choose, always choose
the unknown—because the known you have already lived—never
miss the unknown—always choose the unknown and go headlong—
even if you suffer, it is worth it—it always pays."

—Osho

❧❧❧❧❧ ❧❧❧❧❧

The day I left, he took a bath. He asked if we could make love before
I left for Europe. My mother had been wrong when she'd said, "No
man will ever love you." He loved me deeply, unconditionally. My
mother's words cemented in my subconscious would not allow a
man to love me. He loved me despite the fact that I had never wanted children, despite the infidelities, my unexpected turn to an irrational new career, beginning to modeling at age twenty-five. Now
almost twenty-seven, I rejected him—the supportive, kind, handsome, fun husband. I walked out the door, headed into the next

chapter, leaving everything behind. We did not make love. I was done.

Before leaving for Europe, I had been living in the Bay Area for a year, first with my in-laws in Marin County, until the night they had the fight. My father-in-law stormed out, driving away in their truck to their home near Mount Shasta. His wife (my husband's stepmother) had been a support and a counsel to me as I learned about modeling. Her gorgeous daughter was an aspiring fashion designer. My mother-in-law, Alyce, explained to me that the face was like a canvas that was painted on in modeling. Later, through yoga, another definition of the face came to me: The face is the mirror to the mind. I had never worn makeup until the day that local female photographer had come into Fresno Indian Health, asking if I would model my legs.

The night of the fight between my in-laws, my mother-in-law told me her back was bothering her, that she was going to go get checked at the hospital. When the phone rang at 3:30 a.m., the voice on the other end informed me that Alyce Davidge was dead of metastatic cancer. Had she known? I will never know. It was my first lesson in the fragility of human life, how quickly someone can be gone, how carefully we must handle our battles.

Soon after, I moved in with a young dentist and his wife, renting a room in their Mill Valley home. I was on a wait list for an agency in Paris. I decided not to wait.

With $1000 in my pocket, I departed, leaving the blossoming nutrition career, my healthy marriage. Ron and I had agreed that I would model in Europe for three months. When I had not come back in a year, he sent me divorce papers, asking only that I not use his name. It wasn't until years later, when I saw a letter that my parents had saved from him, that I realized I had left him with the student loans for my master's degree and not honored his request, keeping the name. Donna Davidge was who I had become.

I also left behind a favorite lime-green long sweater jacket, sure that I would replace it with the money from jobs in Europe, only to miss it in particular as I faced the poverty of no work. The $500 business suits I had purchased as a nutritionist, which made me feel like a matron at twenty-six and seemed elaborate yet I could afford them at the time, I naively assumed would be replaced by the beautiful clothes I saw models wearing in magazines. With illusions of grandeur juxtaposed with the dichotomy of a damaged sense of self mired in ego, I took flight to Europe. I was scared, excited, and hopeful that the next step in my dream might come true. The only way to find out was to go.

A gawky tall thin blonde named Susan with big eyes, big lips, and big breasts befriended me at the Grimme agency in San Francisco, the agency that let me go (an awful feeling of rejection at the time) when I said I was going to Paris. Transformed with makeup on, Susan worked a lot in Düsseldorf, Germany. She assured me that I could easily make money in Germany as a push-off point for anything I wanted to do in Europe. Düsseldorf was my destination.

My first modeling job in San Francisco had been for Macy's. They hired me despite the fact that the woman who interviewed me told me I needed a nose job. The small black-and-white photo in the newspaper was stiff, smilingly self-conscious. I never worked for them again. I continued to work on photo "test" shoots in San Francisco to become more comfortable modeling, adding more photos to my portfolio, from which the Paris agency put me on their wait list. Now arrived in Europe, this same insecurity was an obstacle for me to overcome in order to work—to not be stiff and scared of the camera.

I had taken the risk to go on my own to Europe. I was determined, naïve and very scared.

When I got off the plane in Amsterdam, I spoke only English. I didn't know how to change the currency or make a phone call from the airport to find a place to stay. On this European journey, miracles seemed to happen to help me survive, lessons of being open while learning the importance of boundaries. Often trusting strangers in situations that could have turned out very badly, I was just beginning to explore the boundaries of living the unknown accompanied by financial and spiritual poverty.

A young farmer at the airport in Amsterdam, the least expensive city to fly into for European arrival, offered me a cheese sandwich in his limited English, his kindness allaying my anxious feeling of being lost in a world I had no idea how to navigate. My first week in Europe was spent in the small town of Budel with the farmer, who lived with his elderly mother. We went to local pubs, where I met his friends, sharing as much as we could with our language barrier. When it was time for me to move on, he drove me to Düsseldorf, where I had an introduction to a modeling agency through the girl named Susan I had met in San Francisco. The farmer and I said our good-byes. He questioned why I had left a good marriage. I had no answer. I could feel his sadness in his goodbye to me, too. Not fully in touch with my own feelings, I could somehow feel others. My need was to learn how to respond.

I booked a job immediately, which was encouraging. The first few nights, the agency found me a wood floor to sleep on in a pho-tographer's studio. My father had a German friend who worked in journalism in New York City who referred me to a man named Klaus Delauter. Mr Delauter worked for the *Frankfurter Allgemeine* newspa-per. Much to my luck, Mr. Delauter offered me a small apartment on the River Rhine. Mr. Delauter occasionally invited me to breakfast, where I filled myself with thick dark German breads, boiled eggs, and cheese. I combined jam with the cheese, making the enjoyable mixed taste experience of sweet and salty. Mr. Delauter said there was a sadness in my eyes, my feelings still so deeply buried that I could not sense what he saw yet getting subtle messages like his along the way. In an effort to help me, my husband had tried to get me to say the affirming words "I am a reflection of God, which is perfection," something he had learned from his Christian Scientist mother. I had not been able to say them, so damaged was my self-esteem, so fright-ened of the judging devil. To have been told I was going to the devil had instilled a deep-rooted fear about life and myself.

My husband had said he was tired of hearing me complain about my mother. When I had first starved myself to 90 pounds in college (something my mother acknowledged only by bringing me vitamins), I was beginning the slow journey to unearth the self-hatred and shame that blocked the feelings of good in myself. Anorexia is a complex emotional disease that is often linked to the daughter–mother relationship. The wounds ran to a depth that required years of emptying the pus from the wound until it cleared, understanding that parents, my mother, have their own emotional illnesses and their own realities, which can also be harsh and repressed. My lesson was the same many have to learn, that of compassion, understanding, and forgiveness.

After the first job, the Düsseldorf agency got a complaint from the client I had worked for that I had only one smile, the stiff smile of my first job in San Francisco for the Macy's ad. I was not relaxed and fluid, did not really know how to change from one expression, one body expression, to another, nowhere near being over my self-consciousness.

I did not know how to vary my expressions on camera though I was animatedly expressive in life. (A photographer I had interviewed with in San Francisco had said I was better suited to acting because I was animated and expressive, often a nervous response to my self-consciousness.) I froze in front of the camera, adding to my insecurity despite the professional looking photos in my portfolio, taken by patient photographers in San Francisco who had helped me to loosen up, encouraging me with their caring. These were real jobs; this was different than those test shoots where caring photographers helped teach me. I was supposed to know how to do it now. It was traumatizing that I did not know how to relax, so much on the line.

The Düsseldorf modeling agency suggested I get a perm, implying that this might "help" my bookings; my silken hair became a Brillo pad. I looked like a clown, suspecting they had deliberately ruined my straight blond hair to make me quit or move on. I chose to forge ahead, stubborn, independent, determined, and scared shitless. Running home in defeat was not an option. March on with open naive determination I did, knowing in the back of my mind I would not return to the safety of my marriage and prior life. Through my acquaintance with the "other" Donna at the cattle call in Düsseldorf, Paris was my next destination.

***

"Better to have spent a life reaching for a dream that never came true than to have slept through a life that never had a dream."
—Samantha Pickrweign

***

"Twenty years from now you will be more disappointed by the things that you didn't do than by the ones you did do."
—Mark Twain

"The shadow, which is in conflict with the acknowledged values, cannot be accepted as a negative part of one's own psyche and is therefore projected—that is, it is transferred to the outside world and experienced as an outside object. It is combated, punished, and exterminated as "the alien out there" instead of being dealt with as one's own inner problem."

—Erich Neumann in *Depth Psychology and a New Ethic*

My first **professional** modeling picture, taken in San Francisco.

Chapter 12
THE OTHER DONNA & PARIS

While living in Düsseldorf in my first European apartment in 1982,(I was there for six months) the minimal modern apartment Mr. Delauter offered me on the River Rhine, I met a runway model from Boston, also named Donna, at a cattle-call for a show, held in a big hallway with retailers' booths. I offered Donna to stay with me in my apartment, the beginning of a lifelong friendship. Donna, based in Paris, told me that if I ever decided to come to Paris, she would help me. We were opposites—me, natural, not well versed in makeup, fashion, clothes (I often put clothes on inside out or backwards; still do); she, who felt naked without makeup on, a guarded person, especially with men. I was very open socially, both by nature and in searching for self-worth and attention from the outside, especially from men. I was a good girl who had been told she was bad. I was confused, excited, at the same time fearful about the possibilities of experimenting with and experiencing the world far from the research labs of Loma Linda, where I got my master's, far from the woods of New Hampshire, very far from my childhood summers in the woods of Maine. Donna surmised that my openness with men was linked to my love for and from my father, when actually I was testing the cold critical voice of my mother, seeking the attention and warmth I'd never gotten from her.

Adventuresome me persuaded Donna to take nude photos with me in a tub with a German photographer, Manny Lux. Manny had taken me on a trip to Formentera, an island in Spain, with my model friend Susan from San Francisco, Susan getting paid and me getting laid. After I had moved to Paris, he took me to Greece to a Club Med in Kos as his "assistant" while he did a calendar for them based on the theme of family. I was far away from my own family and had no desire to ever create one. In Paris, I would have to make that decision.

A one-night stand with a playboy in Paris who owned a radio station called NRJ made me face the decision of motherhood. I used my contraceptive cream, which had worked every time before. This time I got pregnant, becoming sick 24/7 while I did a much-needed runway job in a department store. NRJ, as I called him, was concerned I would keep the baby; he didn't want the responsibility. My dad happened to call one evening as I lay nauseated on my mattress on the floor of the small room that I shared with a model friend, Shalamee. I told my father I was pregnant. (I am sure this hurt my father, as leaving my marriage had, though he never told me how he felt. I am sure he was more concerned for my welfare than about his feelings. I felt close enough to tell him, never my mother). Though my father and I never discussed this again, at the time I met a model who was very religious like my mother, a kind woman who urged me not to take the life of my unborn child. To this day I feel it was a boy (my sister had two) but will never know. I struggled with the decision, particularly because I met this woman telling me I should keep the child. She said I could move to Texas where there was commercial work for models, start a life and support my child there.

Ultimately, I made the decision that I was in no place emotionally or financially, both accurate instincts, to raise a child. I had never wanted children, even with my adoring well balanced husband, and that never changed. I was not like some models, who latch on to wealthy men by bearing them a child, thus supported. It was not who I was nor wanted to be. NRJ was grateful I made that decision, even checking up on me afterward to make sure I recovered well, which I did.

Years later, while living in New York City, I walked near Radio City Music Hall, watching all the passing businessmen. I thought about how naive I had been in so many ways—the way of business, the way of relationships, the way of dealing with life. These businessmen reminded me of many I had met in Paris, bored with life and bored with their wives, it seemed. They did not have happiness even though they had money. The wide variety of types of men I experimented with prompted my friend Donna to connect me to a journalist in Paris for an article about nymphomania in French *Elle* (which reported that I had a very healthy relationship with sex; was it rebelling or really me? I did not really know). When Dino, my long-term boyfriend in Paris, saw the article, he said that the woman in the article named Maryann was just like me. She *was* me. He knew me that well—my one real boyfriend in Paris, the others just "men." Though our paths diverged, Dino, like Donna, became a lifelong friend.

I had no real intimacy with the man who'd gotten me pregnant. I was willing to give my body away because it was fun and exciting, my libido aroused if someone I found attractive wanted me. In Paris, I would see Madame Claude's high-end call girls at Trocadero, a roundabout filled with outdoor cafés and activity (where I had first met NRJ) sauntering by in their sophisticated beauty. I was told that many of these gorgeous sophisticated women spoke five languages. Even using your body for sex was a competitive market in Europe: Like any "good" job, you needed brains and self-worth.

While I was in Düsseldorf, I had met another model who also lived in Paris—Mary from the Bronx. A man I had met in a bar and hot-tubbed with while living in Mill Valley, California, had given me the name of a friend of his who was Helmut Newton's agent. Newton was a well-known photographer whose specialty was dramatic, erotic fashion photos. His agent asked me to be his date at a castle in Düsseldorf for an event honoring Helmut. (Years later, I would see online that the agent was living in an ashram in California, another to transition from the outer life to the inner.)

At the event, a radiant face with a huge smile popped up to say hello to us. Mary, besides being beautiful, was easygoing, authentic, and lovely. Mary, Düsseldorf Donna, and I became friends. We all booked jobs at the fashion fair, where I had met Donna at the cattle call. I managed to get a job showing lingerie (ironic, as my breasts are small, my athletic body not typical for lingerie modeling), promising the eccentric little man who hired me that I would not get my period that week, a prerequisite for getting the job, which I needed. When I started to bleed, I was sure it was from my rectum, since my period was always regular. I panicked, assuming it must be cancer. (a fear my brother had too but overcame). Donna and Mary accompanied me to the emergency room, the fear welling up inside me, only to discover that I did have my period. I was so out of touch with the body that I easily gave away that I didn't even know what was coming out of where. The stress of needing the job must have prompted my body to sabotage me, a thing I would do to myself in different ways over many years. Looking back, it was quite funny, yet again a lesson from Yogi Bhajan comes to mind: Be aware of what goes in and out of all your holes!

What was possessing me back then? Trying to feel all of life through my adventuresome spirit, feelings so repressed I kept running farther away, unable to accept a hug of condolence from my dietitian best friend back in the States yet randomly having sex with strangers? After three and a half years of craziness in Europe, I would have the good fortune and blessing to encounter Yogi Bhajan. Through his teaching, I would call this phase of my life "looking for love in all the wrong places". My voracious appetite for life was being fed with habits that were actually a crying out that something was wrong. How was I to satisfy the cravings in a healthy way? With no tools yet to change, I partied on.

In the late stages of my living in Europe, around the time I returned to the United States in 1985, AIDS was just coming on the horizon. My father sent me articles on AIDS from the *New York Times* when I came back to New York. I am sure some of the men on my list of 80 had been either bisexual or drug users. This unhealthy sex drive that made me feel so alive was an openness that could also have killed me. The dichotomy of my openness is that it is the same openness that invited Donna to stay in my apartment when we met in Düsseldorf, that open-wide boundary that would continue for years with total strangers, male and female. With people like Donna and Mary, a friendly openness through which I found lasting friendships. Once again I was experiencing the polarity of opposites. Dangerous actions are often covering the angst of fear, substituting behaviors that stem from ignorance and curiosity, actually still burying the feelings that have yet to be resolved. I was reaching for life. Slowly I would evolve better boundaries after years of exposing my body and my self to different people, cultures, and experiences. Yoga would teach me to think of the human body as a container. What did we do with this container? Even if you are blessed, as I was, with an abundance of energy, where do you direct it? How do you learn to contain and direct that energy in healthy ways?

My parents sent me a round-trip ticket to come home for the Christmas holiday/ New Year 1985. I was broken, financially and spiritually bankrupt since I had left the United States. I returned with rich experiences in the shadowy side of sex, (soft) drugs, and a little bit of rock 'n' roll after adventures like a one-night stand with a Rolling Stone and an affair with the Italian drummer from a band I met while they were performing in Tokyo.

I had practiced a lot in front of a camera, much of this practice with my French boyfriend photographer Dino, since my first doomed job for Macy's in San Francisco. In Europe, I was always fearfully anxious about money, where my next meal was coming from. I had written my parents and spoken with them from time to time, always sounding upbeat. I had made fantastic friends, had vast unusual experiences that I never would have had otherwise. It was not until I met my Kundalini yoga teacher in New York city Ravi Singh, who led me to Yogi Bhajan, that I realized the void I was trying to fill was actually the spiritual bankruptcy that yoga and meditation would nourish. When I discovered Kundalini yoga, it was time to move into myself, to look inside for love in all the right places.

In the early '80s, being a model in Paris made it easier to be bohemian—nearly homeless at times, but getting by. Being a model meant invitations to dinner parties, even to Maxim's, the most famous restaurant in Paris. By the time I left Paris, juggling small agencies, I had signed with a small agency called Domina but was still booking no jobs. I had learned that modeling, while often superficial, is actually based on how you see it and let yourself be treated. One famous photographer did tests with me in quiet exchange for sex. I got a few photos out of it. He told me I was "interesting-looking" but not model pretty. He would never think of using me for a job.

Putting my stories, places, and pride behind me, I accepted the ticket from my parents to go back to the States. I would soon be thirty. I was out of money—and pretty much had been for three and a half years—when I landed in New York City, near my parents, who still lived in my childhood home in Stamford, Connecticut. Starting over once again, this time, for lack of a better choice, in the Big Apple. My mother thought I should go back to dietetics, but I had let my Registered Dietitian license lapse. My lifestyle had completely changed to that of the unconventional "artist." I decided to keep that seed going, though I didn't know how. My first New York City roommate (I shared a tiny studio and bunk beds with him) was the boyfriend of a female photographer I'd met in Paris. One day while I was out jogging in Washington Square Park, he went into my suitcase, stealing the last $500 I had to my name. Now I literally had nothing.

I ended up choosing to live in Manhattan after a trip to the city to stay for a weekend with Düsseldorf/Paris Mary and her boyfriend for my thirtieth birthday January 15. It was 1985. Mary added hot milk to the coffee, reminding me of the rich, steaming, strong coffees of Paris, where she and I had continued our friendship after meeting in Germany. I had been passionately committed to the modeling, doing lots of test shoots and go-sees in Paris. I continued to do that in New York, now with European shots in my portfolio. Not many of the shots were from actual jobs, though my French boyfriend, Dino, had finally gotten me my dream of being in *Vogue* right before I left Europe: It was a profile for a clothing ad with my hair covering my eyes so that all you saw was my nose (the nose that needed surgery, according to the Macy's woman from my first job in San Francisco). The photographer's suggestion that I would be better off acting than modeling returned to my thoughts. I had remembered the photographer's words while I was modeling in Japan, the two most lucrative months of my modeling career, except I never saw any money from my work in Japan when I got back to my agency in Paris.

In New York I got representation from an agency called Click for commercials, of course slept with my agent, which felt awful and awkward. (Didn't I know by now that this would NOT advance anything?) He was young and cute, but there was no connection on any level. A cocoon is toxic until it becomes a butterfly. As long as I was in my cocoon, I could be of no use to anyone in an intimate relationship. I was beginning to realize that lack of connection led to nothing professionally; on a personal level, these encounters were like a butterfly's cocoon, toxic, no way ready to transform into a thing of fragile beauty like the butterfly, the image I had loved since my early twenties and would fill the Sewall House with.

Click did provide me with my first acting coach, an Italian-American actor named Tony. Our small class met a few times. We sat in metal folding chairs. When Tony asked me to sit in front of the others, I literally twisted my legs and arms around each other (like a yoga pose called eagle), my body language so closed. I had spent three years in Europe trying to have the courage to open up, to expose my self, but only doing so in the privacy of promiscuity or in the nude photos taken in Europe. Inside I was still removed from my feelings, my self. Yoga would heal these complexes, heal the wounds, without the crutches of drugs, alcohol, or sex. In France, my boyfriend Dino had put up with so much, as had my husband before him, including the time I broke it off with Dino, running off to southern France with a French artist (who did a painting of me I wish I had today). This prompted Dino to follow me there to propose marriage. I turned him down. I lived through all this, what Yogi Bhajan called emotion commotion. My soul cried for a change.

The return to the United States in 1985 drew me back to my roots. I met my Kundalini yoga teacher through a woman I met in passing when out for drinks with a group. The stage manager for the Paul Taylor Dance Company had taken over the bunk bed of the young man who stole my last $500. He was hip and attractive; we slept together; he invited me out for drinks with some friends. The scrap of paper the woman gave me that night with Ravi Singh's phone number changed my life, just as a trip to Island Falls, Maine, had changed the course of a young Theodore Roosevelt's life.

In addition to finding yoga while living in my first living situation in New York City, I found my first professional acting coach through the woman whose boyfriend stole my last $500 from that apartment. Ed Kovens, a student of renowned acting teacher Lee Strasburg, the method acting teacher who had taught many, including Marilyn Monroe, taught me to act. I never observed Ed's womanizing reputation I heard of; no womanizer compared to all those I had seen and been with in Europe. He was a great teacher, slightly crass; his young girlfriend Jill, who was in our class, would become his wife. For three and half years, I committed to Ed's classes, which developed into a close-knit group of aspiring actors. One went on to Hollywood, getting his break on the TV show *Melrose Place*. The method acting technique tears you open as you recall personal experiences to create the emotions for acting. Acting unlocked long-repressed feelings as I learned how to feel the depths of pain through tears, instead of pushing people away. Without learning to cry, I don't think I could really live fully or love. I had pushed people away from true closeness and caring, people like my first husband and my best friend during my dietetic internship. Having not learned as a child to be comforted, I did not know how to comfort; having not been hugged or shown physical affection, I did not know how to show affection. The sexual experiences I had been exploring were a false way of demonstrating closeness, a way to run away from true intimacy.

The Kundalini yoga I was learning from Ravi was the healing fix. I jogged forty-five minutes from the upper west side apartment I was now living in to lower east Manhattan in the early morning to attend his seven a.m. classes for $5, often going back to the noon classes Ravi offered me for free.

I began looking for acting jobs through the trade newspaper Backstage. I met the young B-film maker (Gorman) on an open call who created a part for me—a neurotic, high-strung young woman, Heather. I did a hilarious monologue on how yoga kept her from suicide. Heather is wound up very tight, funny, geeky and attractive (me at the time!). I had just recently done a modeling job that dyed my hair platinum for a hair magazine. I needed the $300, a before-and-after where my European-styled super-short hair was dyed. The job was done by Frederic Fekkai, whom I had met in Europe in informal social situations; Frederic was a rising star in the hair world. (I would later get to stand in for Cybil Shepherd in a L'Oreal with another "arrived" young makeup artist, Kevin Aucoin, who would transform my face. He passed away at too young an age, but there is still a makeup line bearing his name.)

> "WAKE UP! Today I choose life. Every morning when I wake up, I can choose joy, happiness, negativity, pain… To feel the freedom that comes from being able to continue to make mistakes and choices—today I choose to feel life, not to deny my humanity but embrace it."
>
> —Kevyn Aucoin on Facebook, 2015

Gorman, the young filmmaker of his own film company, Generic Films, loved platinum hair. He was a Hitchcock fan; Hitchcock had also favored light blondes. My platinum hair helped me become a favorite of Gorman's for a while. He put me in two more movies with good parts, then the parts got crappier. His films did not help my career, though a good agent told me the comedic monologue as

Heather in the movie *Psychos in Love* showed my talent. Gorman and I practiced and practiced. The monologue was done in one take. In modeling and acting, I was not selective, taking any job for the experience. I was grateful to work, even if the venue was lousy. I had done things in Europe like the cover of a girlie magazine, taking any job that would pay any money. Gorman's movies were cult films about sex, young women, and nudity. I had a leading part in the first movie I shot for him, called *And Then*, which included nudity. It never showed anywhere. I also did student and low-budget films that are not to be found anywhere today. I received a $6 annual residual check from Paramount for a nonspeaking part in the movie, *Tales from the Darkside*. I continue to pay annual dues to the acting unions.

While the chosen few get there, my "someday" star in modeling and acting was not to come. I eventually landed a manager, an attractive fiftyish woman who believed in me. She suggested that I needed self-confidence. Still that! (When I worked as a stand-in in *Pet Sematary*, the casting director said that often the choice during casting came down to an actor's self-confidence.) My manager suggested therapy, which I did for a few years with a woman in the West Village. The female therapist had worked with Steven Spielberg's wife (they were still friends) before she was his wife. She said that she saw similarities between me and Kate—both of us came to acting late with a master's degree in something else. Kate, in contrast, became a paid working actress (and married Spielberg!). I did work some, often for little or no pay. I looked the therapist up in the spring of 2012, discovering she had passed away. Ten years older than me, she had thought buying Sewall House was a stupid idea. It seemed strangely ironic that I was still alive, meeting the challenges of doing the thing she had thought would not work. Even if I had had the money to invest in New York City, as she suggested, purchasing the Sewall House was never a financial investment. It was a decision from the heart and soul.

My acting manager got me some decent auditions. I got into all the acting unions, including the Screen Actors Guild, (SAG) another stroke of luck that happened because my face was seen in the opening scene of the movie BIG. A commercial in San Francisco made before I moved to Europe prequalified me for the union, unbeknownst to me. When my face appeared in a scene at the opening of the film BIG, I got into SAG, (Screen Actors Guild Union) which led to tons of extra work on many movies. I could finally afford rent and the acting classes in NYC, both of which my parents had paid until I got on my feet, embarrassing but necessary after returning with nothing to show for my time in Europe but a portfolio of modeling photos, and the $500 that was stolen.

I started acting when I was thirty. By the time I hit forty, I had been acting in a stream of off-off-Broadway plays for the "experience" (no pay), especially with Love Creek, a not-very-high-profile but prolific theater group (I directed one play with them before leaving acting), but no career "break" was imminent. I studied acting with the actor Michael Moriarty, who taught small groups out of his home before he became a cast member on *Law and Order*. I studied acting five days a week for eight weeks in a summer program at Neighborhood Playhouse. My most memorable teacher at Playhouse was a gay man named Richard Pinter. Richard Pinter is the reason I read *War and Peace*. He pranced into class the first day, very lively, and asked us all why we wanted to act. After hearing the varied answers, he said, "You are acting for one of two reasons: You either want to give love or get love." He spoke of Tolstoy's love for writing, how on his deathbed he was writing in the air with an imaginary pen, an example of the passion required by artists.

At Neighborhood Playhouse, when I was thirty-three, I choreographed a dance to *Phantom of the Opera*. I had seen and loved the play with my well-to-do businessman boyfriend at the time, Jeffrey, when it first hit Broadway. Jeffrey had been married to a well known Hollywood producer's daughter for twenty-eight years. I was a breath of fresh air for him. He was a stabilizing influence for me, another gift through Kundalini yoga. He was my first private student. I studied Shakespeare with a British woman in her eighties named Ada Brown Mather. She was tough. I was terrible. She wrote me after she moved back to England that she felt I could do anything I wanted if I put myself into it. We kept in touch through letters after I changed my life direction once again. A career in acting, which seemed like winning the lottery, was not happening.

Michael Moriarty urged all his acting students to write a one-person show. I created "In This, Our Home," writing an imagined dialogue between Mary, my dead great-grandmother, and very alive me to see if she could offer any insights into life, the thing I was trying to make sense of. I spent a year working with a director from the Love Creek Theater Company on the piece, weekly meetings of rewrites and rehearsals. I had two staged readings, one at HB Acting Studios, where I taught Kundalini yoga, and the other at a tiny theater I rented on Madison Avenue. A dozen supportive friends and students came, including the lovely British man I was dating seven years after Jeffrey. I was now forty.

After the reading was over, the director said he was disappointed in me. I asked why. (that eternal question again). He replied, "Until you got up and read the script on stage, I never understood what a good actor you were." The best scene, he said, had been me sitting in a chair portraying my great-grandmother close to death in childbirth (birthing her second child, my dear Uncle Fred, who became known as the badlands baby) from the intense August heat at Theodore Roosevelt's Elkhorn Ranch in North Dakota. Interesting that I did that so well, since I had never wanted or had the experience of childbirth.

At the time of the reading, my boyfriend was a funny, good-hearted man from England who worked in publishing (Bibles). He attended the reading as well as Aunt Nancy's 100th birthday party in Island Falls. Tall Paul, wavy brown hair and a beard; it seemed logical that he was a good salesman because everyone liked him. I had met him while out for drinks with a travel agent that an Irish friend from my acting class and I were meeting before a ten-day trip to Ireland. After nine months with him, I broke up with the fabulous Brit for a not-so-fabulous writer I'd met on my last paid acting job, an industrial (actors putting on skits at conventions) for Ford in Palm Springs. That relationship was very short-lived. Despite ten years of Kundalini yoga, there were healthier parts of me that yet needed to be uncovered.

My living situation had improved (sort of) since the $500 had been stolen from my suitcase at my first New York City rental apartment. I'd moved in with an eccentric professor, bunking on his sofa for $100 a month, (crazy low rent with three stipulations- make his bag lunches, be in no later than 10pm, give him nonsexual massages, quirky professor; for that rent I did it). My next move was to a futon on the floor in a small room off the kitchen in a large apartment on the Upper West Side with a German woman who was a Shiatsu massage therapist, from which I jogged down to Ravi's lower

East side yoga classes every morning. In 1988, I finally got my own legal sublet in Little Italy through a friend in Ed's acting class. The apartment was one (dark) room, tub in the kitchen, like many old New York City apartments. I had my own pad at last. After two years, in 1990, when the owner came back to his apartment on Spring Street in Little Italy, I found another sublet through a man in the neighborhood, "Butchie the hat." I knew Butchie through extra work on movies, where he always wore a different hat. His grandmother had died, one of those rare good-luck New York City rental stories. The apartment was full of Madonna statues, evidence of having been lived in by a devout Catholic, and two beds with worn-out mattresses. Despite the strange feeling of the place I had my own apartment! In a historic run-down building in Little Italy, this one offered more room (and light) than my first sublet in the same neighborhood. I lived alone in this 590-square-foot railroad apartment until I bought Sewall House, taking a roommate at the time I bought the house, 1997, to help me be able to afford the (albeit not huge) mortgage on the house. I found the apartment's cracked walls and uneven floors charming. Butchie's mom, who lived with him and his brother in the apartment underneath me, eventually allowed me to get rid of some of the old furniture. I kept the solid antique bedroom set, painted the hallway of the apartment yellow, doing what I could to make it reflect me. When the city decided to renovate the building (in 2000), I qualified as a legal tenant in a rent-stabilized situation, providing ten years of tax returns showing low income, the income of an aspiring actress and yoga instructor just barely getting by.

Despite working hard, being told by certain professionals that I had what it took in both modeling and acting, the acting career was stalled. Kundalini yoga was the thread that helped me continue to evolve, slowly the caterpillar urging its way out of the cocoon. In my first marriage, I had butterflies on the napkins and match covers, not knowing this represented fragility and transformation. My shell was gradually peeling away so the "good heart" that my photographer friend Tony in Paris told me I had would begin to unfold. Time and time again, I was carried forward by the kindness of some stranger. Underneath my apparent self-centered seeking, kindness and gratitude reflected back.

Chapter 13
BAD LUCK OR GOOD?
Sexploitations & Sexcapades

First used in the 1600s: **pro·mis·cu·ous** (prə-´mis-kyə-wəs) *adj.*

1. characterized by or having numerous sexual partners on a casual basis.
2. consisting of a disordered mixture of various elements.
3. indiscriminate; without discrimination.
4. casual; irregular; haphazard.

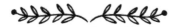

When I was twelve years old, my friend Sue and I somehow got hold of a paperback book called *Call Me Brick*. I have no idea why that was the title. All I know is that it had explicit sensuous descriptions of lovemaking. While my hormones were rising, the confusion of my repressed upbringing and the sexual attention I had received inappropriately at a young age did not feel or seem like the luscious descriptions in this book. We would pour over various sections, giggling in my room, then hide it away in my bedroom drawer.

By the time I left my first marriage, I had not explored a lot sexually. I'd lost my virginity at age twenty to my patient, loving boyfriend from high school who attended a college not so far from me in New Hampshire. I had a few boyfriends in college after breaking up with the high school boyfriend, who was hoping to marry me (and went on to become a Congregational minister and marry his next girlfriend). My first husband and I had a healthy sexual relationship based on fun mutual attraction. EST, the narcissistic catalyst for my jumping off, combined with my exploration into modeling, caused it all to shift. The opportunities to have casual sex in the modeling world are frequent if you want it or are naive or insecure enough to give into it. As a model, I defined myself as a free (open-legged) spirit. I doubt anyone who had known me in high school or college would have expected that from me if they knew me in my wholesome achievement-oriented younger years. I had always been friendly and outgoing but not jumping into any beds. I was groomed for a life direction that running off to Europe gave me the freedom to change.

I did not sleep with just anyone. I was selective in my adventures, but because the opportunities were everywhere, there were many encounters. Sometimes I would sleep with a photographer because he was well known. With some, there was an unspoken communication that they would not do photos for an unknown model like me unless they thought you had true potential or, if not, that there was something in it for them—sex. For example, a well known Parisian photographer who told me I was "interesting-looking" did several test shoots with me, including one where he draped a transparent black cloth over my face, another where I sat in a chair in a simple evening gown with my legs open, my head held up to the sky with my eyes closed. The most expressive photo he took of me was in a black short skirt and a one-piece top thing sprawled on a bed with my head turned to the side, staring into space with a sad, haunting expression on my face. The exchange for the photos was sex. Every time.

Of the more memorable "sexations," was when my photographer friend Tony set me up with a Rolling Stone. The Rolling Stones had just spent six months on an island recording. All I remember about the dinner was South American musicians coming by strumming their instruments by our table and the rock star saying, "These are the real musicians." I really did not know who this musician I was having dinner with was. My French boyfriend at the time was a huge Mick Jagger fan who still goes to their concerts around the world. He may have been more jealous of the fact that I was out with a Stone than he was concerned about whether I would sleep with him, which of course I did, mainly out of curiosity.

A small modeling agency got me to Tokyo, taking all my earnings for the two months I worked there. I never saw a cent from the lucrative market that was Japan modeling in the '80s. I moved on, I thought upward, to other agencies. Though I never got a job, I did get more sex. My second agency was owned by a wealthy playboy who would go on to marry a wealthy heiress not too long after my interlude with him. That marriage surprised me because he had beautiful girlfriends and models all around him. I guess at that time he liked money even more than beautiful women. The weekend after I was accepted into the agency a few new models were invited to the agency owner's "castle" in the French countryside for the weekend.

On Saturday afternoon, the handsome model agency owner asked if I wanted to go on a scooter ride. We ended up at his father's estate nearby, alone in the indoor swimming pool having sex. By the time I got home Sunday evening, my boyfriend Dino, who knew me all too well, had put my belongings in a locker at the bus station. More drama. The agency owner put me up in his apartment, where I had my own room across from his with a living room in between. He was busy with his life, asking me one day to leave because his Italian girlfriend was coming, but not before he had a wild dinner party night, with wine and cocaine flowing. Fourteen-year-old girls who had just gotten off the plane were invited. I ended up in his bedroom, where I noticed he had my modeling composite photo on his mantel. When he asked me that night to have sex with his friend, a good-looking married man, I stopped at that. I returned to Dino. As my boyfriend, he did not like it; as an open-minded European, he accepted it.

Another memorable experience happened the night I was invited to dinner by a long-haired blond backgammon player I had slept with once or twice. Ostensibly, we were going to dinner at a restaurant in Paris with some film producers. We drove to the restaurant but were told to stay in the car as they loaded food into the trunk. We proceeded to a home in the countryside where we were wined, dined and filled with pot. There was a voluptuous blonde giving men oral sex in the corner of the room by the long table where we were eating, drinking, and smoking. I retreated as far as I could, finding a small room upstairs where the backgammon boy came, had sex with me, then left. I was there all night, delivered disheveled and hung over the next morning by one of the few sleazy men still there in the morning when I awoke. It was a frightfully dreadful night, especially because I could not get back to my boyfriend and did now even know where we were.

Work assignments were few and far between. I took a job in Istanbul for one weekend to show dresses to private buyers. The man who got me the job was a short, balding, big-bellied American who sleazed around getting independent jobs. The gray-haired bearded Frenchman with a bulbous nose who hired me directed me to go through customs with several of the same dresses in different sizes in my luggage (that he would sell to his clients in Turkey). My employer was as sleazy as the man who had gotten me the job. What he was asking me to do was illegal entry with goods with the intent to sell. I could have been arrested. He told me, "If they ask anything, just tell them you are a model and these are your clothes" (which they did). When the old man who hired me to go to Istanbul with him snuck into my room to see if I would give in to him, I strongly said in my best French, "*Jai chaleureux*," which I thought meant *I am angry* (colore) but meant *I am hot*. Even with my comical mistake, he got the message. The highlight of this job was seeing Istanbul, a beautiful city. We visited an elegant home of one of his connections, filled with rich fabrics and furniture. Modeling was a world where you could have nothing yet be in the most expensive homes and restaurants in the world, contrasting your pauper's existence.

The comical crab story didn't feel that way at the time. I accepted a summer job through the *International Herald Tribune* with a wealthy older Greek interior designer who owned a home in Switzerland near the home of the Shah of Iran. His girlfriend, so he said, was incapacitated for a while so he wanted someone to travel with. For a couple of weeks, we night clubbed, did Lake Cuomo and the Swiss Alps, where I loved hiking in the astounding nature. The heights gave him anxiety attacks, which I helped him through simply by being there (premonition of my future life in the healing arts?). We became friends. I had no desire to have sex with him, which might have earned me more money. Lucky for him we did not engage in the act, as the little spiders I found in my pubic hair he was sure had come from the forests would have been transmitted to him.

I went to a doctor who told me *au contraire;* I had contracted crabs. I washed with the medicinal soap, the itchy tiny creatures disappeared. The darn crabs reappeared when I returned to Paris and slept again with my friend Frank, a businessman from the U.S. who had let me stay in his company flat on Pont Neuf when he was away for a month. He took me to a weekend in Amsterdam. When I saw the critters reappear, obviously from him, I lay back on the bed, demanding that he shave me then and there to get rid of the tiny creeping itchy things he had given me.

Gonorrhea was another story; I had no idea from whence or whom that came. All I knew was that my body felt drained. Normally blessed with a high level of energy, in Paris my life my energy directed mainly into sexuality and photo test shoots in hopes of work. The passionate spirit that usually drove me was feeling uncharacteristically exhausted. When I went to the doctor, he held a mirror so I could see the lesion in my vagina, evidence that promiscuity is definitely not a healthy thing even if *Marie Claire* surmised in their article on nymphomania that I had a healthy attitude toward sex.

What I did have was a guardian angel: Between the naive legal risk at customs in Istanbul and the unconscious risks I was taking with my sexuality I did not get arrested—or AIDS.

Photo: Parisian photographer

Photo: Parisian photographer

Photo: Parisian photographer

■ May 25, 2005 Before Heading to Maine

I lie in bed with my left buttock half exposed under the comforter. The subtle soft sweep of my cat Westy's tail invites me to awaken to the slow sensual tapping of his caressing tail. My tail has been exposed to much in its fifty years of living. This morning my tail is glad to greet the tameness of this tail's message to me—the belt from childhood, the slap of the billionaire's stinging hand to excite him: *You can slap me, but even with some cocaine in me, I will not do your friend. You can belt me, but you cannot break my spirit.*

Chapter 14
NOTES FROM THE '80S
—Jagged Beginnings in the Big Apple & Inching Toward a Yogi Solution

■ **Restless Wanderings, August 29, 2013**

Christmas holiday of 1984/5, I was turning thirty, the big 3-0, in January. Three and a half years before, my father had spent an hour on the phone, encouraging me to stay in the States, to stick with my marriage. My dad was now encouraging me to return to "use the inside of my head," which *he* did so exceptionally well. I was grateful to go home though still unsure of my direction. Europe had distanced me from my parents. I had kept in touch, acting as though life was good when often it was frighteningly uncertain.

Living in Paris had shaped me in its distance from the life that had been expected of me. European living offered beautiful moments—visiting outdoor markets after my morning runs, going to outings with friends in the countryside, enjoying simple dinner parties of salads with the kitchen sink thrown in at our Les Halles apartment (rent usually paid by my younger boyfriend Dino's supportive mother) juxtaposed with dinner invitations to fancy oh-so-French restaurants that came as a perk of being a model, successful or not. Jobs to Istanbul and Morocco for the weekend. Club Meds in Greece and Morocco. Parties in our apartment filled with friends, wine and pot, affairs and one-night stands, the uncertainty exciting and exhilarating, jumping full force into experiences so different from any I'd had before. I believed that being in front of cameras would help me lose my self-consciousness, as if this world based on external physical beauty could make me overcome my feeling of ugliness inside.

EST had compelled me to leave Ron. From the little girl doing toothpaste commercials in front of the mirror to Ron's young K.O. wife, who disliked mirrors immensely, the words prevailed: "No man will ever love you"—feeling the demons within, making me feel ugly, still unlovable. Kundalini yoga entered my life, an inner journey with eyes closed, energy felt moving inside. I had come home to a place inside me that could rearrange these deep feelings of shame and unworthiness. Ron made the first step with me, more than he would ever know, when he asked me to repeat those words he'd learned from his mother—*I am a reflection of God, which is perfection*—but I could not say them then. Yoga would help me to get there.

Tony, an American photographer living in Paris, introduced me to a woman who arranged sex with men. Tony thought Susie might find a husband to take care of me but that was not the way I wanted to do things. I was still searching for me. Tony took a few beautiful portrait photos of me. He and I had a memorable, one-time moment of sex. Much more memorable were the telling words about my "good heart"* that I have ruminated on for years, coming to peace with the wounds, as we all need to, and accepting the round-trip ticket to go back and face the dregs of what little was left of what I'd left behind, no marriage or career to greet me on the other side.

* "You have a good heart but someone did a number on it."

■ Notes from New York in the '80s

"There will be many chapters in your life. Don't get lost in the one you are in now."

—Quote on Instagram, June 12, 2015.

As I reread notes of lost moments, this quote seems perfect (moments of being lost?). What follows is a series of fragments written in my early days in New York City in the mid- to late-1980s, anger seeping through at the same time as my vivid living in the city. My language is rougher, even vulgar; I look at how it evolved away from that so much that seventeen years later, one of my first yoga students said, "Remember how you used to swear?" No, I don't (until I see these notes). Yikes! How unconscious was I?

Behind the closed doors within the walls of a family lurk the demons of dysfunction. In their complexity, humans can well hide, which further buries the very things that need to be surfaced to begin the healing, the change that will discontinue the cycle.

"What you resist persists."
—Carl Jung/Werner Earhart,
EST founder

■ March 7, late 1980s

Sirens shrieking, the constant drone of the city. Drown it out with Lou Reed [who just passed away a few weeks ago as I type in 2013 what I wrote in a notebook in the 1980s]. My day starts at 5 a.m., startled awake from a deep dream. Why can't I recall my active dream life more clearly? Get up to sense the cold, pull on long johns and sweatpants. Maybe one day it would be cool to be irresponsible, to just get up and get fucked up. God, what an attitude. I hear young girls kidding on the subway using the f-word like we use our breath. I am like that, oh God! I will make a conscious effort to curb it.

Out the door, leave a light on, apartment broken into not so long ago. [If *that* didn't feel like a violation!] Descent to hell, the subway at 5:30 a.m. This morning there is a young guy with glazed eyes, he comes out of nowhere, swearing and kicking the wall. Where has he been all night? A whacky man with gray hair starts talking with him. The young man responds with such anger that the gray-haired homeless man walks away.

It is a relief to step off the crazy platform into the subway car to watch the tired people going to or coming from work. I arrive at my client's. She is more awake than usual. We pass the hour quickly, talking about her business colleague dying of AIDS. *I want to fly*, says Lou Reed. I get so angry that I am sad. I can't get in touch.

I want to express myself, so I buy this composition notebook because I came to NY to act, cannot seem to get where I want to go, so I start to read the Bible, teach yoga, all trying to make me grow, get in touch. Patience is a virtue. I pray. Another day is over. Another day starts.

I can't ever discuss my deep dark feelings because they are not clear. Where are they? What are they? What am I afraid of? Smidgens of those dreams—goddammit it, I want to catch them. I want to get on with it. I have been through so much. It is only 7 a.m. I am so weary.

■ March 8

What a difference! Today I see the sunshine, I feel the bitter cold. The demons are on sabbatical. Let them stay there. Soon they will retire, travel to a far-off land. This body no longer needs or desires them. Coming from love is best, I'm OK. I am more than OK. People touch my life. Pray for the homeless, those who bug you. Be yourself. In silence, there is strength. Two angels sent from God last night. I turned around. They were gone, sent in such a deceiving form; two teenage boys, one black and one white, yin and yang, positive and negative. Dreams about unfulfilled friendships. Potential popping up. Correct attitude. Clear up your life. Clean up your apartment and your pocketbook. Success is not only material gain. Virtue, give. Look inside yourself to blame and grow, outside yourself to give and know. Afraid of feeling, afraid of showing myself, no fear, no fear, no fear.

The other night, I got out of a play rehearsal after a gray drizzly day. A young man in the cast and I decide to catch the subway together. We descend into what I affectionately [not] call hell [an indicator of some anger and association with that descending image of the devil my mother planted in my mind]. The subway feels like the bowels of the city. The sign pointing to our underpass leads us to an endless set of stairs that are a nonfunctioning escalator. At the bottom of the stairs are several oversized rats running around. My companion says, "No. Come on, we'll just swipe them away." Three-fourths of the way down, we realize it's marked off with dainty ribbons, of all things. I run up the stairs exclaiming, "I should have married the millionaire!" I realize this is his wedding day. I am crawling around in the dungeon while he is breaking glasses with his feet on his wedding day.

The next day, I am leaving my $650-dollar-a-month antiquated apartment (the first solo one)with bathtub in the kitchen, dark though it is several flights up, to teach yoga (finally found a sublet where I can live alone and afford it). The key won't turn, as usual. Force has worked so far, but this time it breaks, stuck in the lock. Having left a message to the landlord asking him to fix the lock earlier that day, I walk down to see if he is in. "Why didn't you tell me about the lock sooner?" he asks. I did! We ramble back up the flights of stairs and he says, "Just in case, how about access through your window if we cannot get in the door?" I remind him that the apartment was broken into in February so now we have bars on the window. He bursts the door open; not reassuring to see how easy he can do that. He gets the key out, unscrews the whole shebang, puts it back together, tries the door, it won't lock. He fools with the door connection and it works like a gem. As he is trotting down the stairs, I call to him, "Marlowe, it's not working easy," as I try it. He calls back without a glance, "Keep trying, it will."

I call the health club to tell them I will be late to teach and descend again into hell. My train pulls out. Typical. I wait fifteen minutes for the next local, a million expresses pass. I am reading my book with my elbows so I can cover my ears each time the noise machine clamors by. I finally arrive at the class half an hour late. Three people waited. "You lost four," a man quips.

I turn to the class with my broken key and explain, "God said 'fuck you' tonight."

"What did you say?" asks one lady. [Obviously not what you expect from the mouth of a yoga teacher. The years of practice whittled this habit away, thank God; I was a newbie when this happened, struggling to survive New York.)

Oh boy, just another day in New York City.

The young black man looms over me. I am napping on the subway on a tedious trip to a tedious job, a three-night shoot in Harlem. (more film extra work) The heat is on. He has a leather necklace of Africa around his neck, good strong features on a handsome face. As the train pulls out into the daylight, the sun hits the curly hair on his legs in a way that makes his skin glimmer, a glowing chocolate color. The train stops. The door opens. I bolt out toward my destination, leaving behind the image and memory of a stranger.

■ July 28, 1989

The alarm goes off. *Brrrring!* What for? It is still dark out. Oh yeah, the Kundalini yoga sadhana, the 3:30 am practice we did every morning in New Mexico at my first solstice retreat there. [I would go to the next ten and then two more.]

I promised to join my teacher, Ravi, to do the sadhana today [it is a yoga practice with chanting, but new to it, I call it a ceremony]. The alarm is ringing at 4:10 a.m. on a Saturday morning, four hours of sleep. [The first time, I did it in the dessert in June, waking up at 3:30 a.m. I felt like lead.] Should I go? Shouldn't I?

I slump across the room to turn the overhead light on. It doesn't switch on with the first try. Is that an omen to go back to bed? The light goes on with a boom the second time. I look at my face in the mirror and look amazingly awake. I pull on some shorts; the room is hot. Out into the early a.m. air I go, surprisingly cool; a shift in weather had been predicted.

Walking up Lafayette Street toward Astor Place at 4:30 a.m. is not the most protected feeling in the world. A not-so-hungry-sized rat scurries across the sidewalk just south of Houston. I will be glad to be in the woods next week, visiting my parents at the cabin in Maine where I spent my childhood summers. *Ad Guray Nameh*, the gurus' chant for protection.

I see a group of punks walking home from somewhere, but mostly I see homeless and junkies. I avert my eyes, walk purposefully ahead, ignoring comments. I arrive at Astor Place finally, to my destination at 9th Street and 4th Avenue. I yank, yank, yank on the door. Locked. I am chilly, underdressed in my shorts and sleeveless top. A homeless man is sitting a few stoops down. He has one of those shopping carts filled with nondescript plastic bags, not dressed too shabbily or too dirty. He approaches me timidly and asks if I have a cigarette. "Sorry," I say sincerely, "I don't smoke."

He backs off, and I lay my head on my knees as my tiredness still permeates my body. I shift, having forgotten the bum. A few minutes later, he approaches, a little closer this time. He asks me if I would like a coffee. "Are you OK?" he asks with seemingly real concern. "I thought maybe you were sick or something."

"No, thank you, I am fine; just waiting for some people who have not arrived yet."

He retreats again, into the background, forgotten.

My friends arrive 1-2-3. We go inside for the sadhana. When I come out two hours later, the man is gone. The sky is light; it is day. His memory lingers. I am touched. Who was this man? Why was he here? Neither of us will know each other's story. For those few moments, a genuine connection was felt, a concern for a fellow human being who, for whatever reason, has far less than I. Yet he was willing to help me. The mysteries in this city, never to be solved, left only a story to elaborate in my imagination.

■ Fragments of My Life in the Mid-1980s, Newly Arrived in New York City

I gave Cary Grant three sleeping pills. He died. I had to live with that. I remove the evidence, pages from a journal, some paychecks, one of my boots. I go to a community center, trying to climb to the ladies' room, but it was dangerous so I couldn't get up there. I went to get some material for a writer, but there was a psycho there so I hid. He found me and had pliers to kill me. These are my dreams when I first arrive in New York.

This is my reality. I am sitting next to a man on the subway platform who is desperately repeating, "Where is the beauty in life? In a flower, in a poem; it is not like they said it would be. Truth is beauty, beauty is truth, truth is beauty. But there are no flowers with parks like in Paris." This man is out of it but I don't move away. I listen, he repeats the same thing over and over, I look around. He is right. All around us is cement and steel. This is spring. Where are the flowers? I feel as if something is missing. *God is great, God is good*, my mother says at the dinner table. I am locked in the attic. It feels like she is going to kill me no matter what. Mother leaves me with him. I tell her what he does to me. She will never leave me with him again. These experiences are there, embedded, even as I sit on a subway many years later listening to the musings of a madman.

I'm teaching a class. I look out the window and see the cars crawling down FDR Drive like insects, busy ants working on their hill.

I am cracking up. I need to see the forest.

We are sitting in the cabin playing Scrabble; the lightning lights up the lake every few seconds. It is a monster storm. This is the time we see the lightning walk itself right into the tree twenty feet from our cabin, split-second action, burning brightly and long it seems—a crackle, then water pours from the heavens, arresting the sparks traveling toward the woodshed. I look at him, I look at Father, I look at Mother. My God, she has actual tears in her eyes, tears of fear. I have never seen a tear in her eye. Nature speaks; nature moves us. We should listen.

How easy it was to pass the hours with my dolls Barbie and Ken on the rocks, the waves lapping at my feet, every puddle their swimming pool. How much I learned from that forest. And Cary Grant really is dead.

■ August 4: Now I Am in the Forest/Contrast to the Craziness of New York City

First day in the forest
Pitch darkness of the forest
Pitter-patter of rain on the tin roof
Eternal quietness
The loon's lullaby
Here once again
To luxuriate in meditate
Facing oneself
Uncontrollable laughter
Till tears come into the eyes
How pure is humor
How essential is laughter and song

BROTHER: Can't do anything for himself. Helpless, must get others involved in his drama. Where is this? Where is that? Never takes the half second it takes to find anything. He narrates his life so negatively. I can't do this. I can't do that. Can someone help me with this and that? ("Can your can't" —Yogi Bhajan).

Totally non-self-sufficient. Where he is in this is safe for him. Always playing the victim. The world is persecuting him. If something feels threatening, he has an anxiety attack. His mind chatter-

chatters. He lets his mind take over. All of these things I see in my-self are magnified in him. He makes no effort to reach within as I have been doing with Kundalini yoga. Yogi Bhajan: "Never say I don't know, I can't, I'm not ready." Eliminate these from the mind, constant practice. Break habits if you really want to let go of the misery.

His mornings are rough. His stomach is killing him. He has a good brain, soft heart, sensitivity. Where did it go wrong? He is so defeated. I wish I could do it for him, but I can't. It is all so clear now. I will do the best I can. I will be responsible.

MOTHER: She comes down the stairs, swirls across the cold li-noleum floor, holding her pajama legs up like an elegant skirt, moving like a little girl. I smile up from my cot, say, "Hi, Mom," but she doesn't hear me. She hasn't put her hearing aid on yet. The little girl I have imagined becomes my seventy-nine-year-old mother, her chin length gray hair askew from her night of sleep. The sun is seeping through the trees. It is 6 a.m., our first real day of sunlight to awaken us since arriving last week. I slip out into the sunshine to find the canoe, to look for the deer I spotted last evening when I rode along with my mother while she read to me about the poverty of Ethiopia. We shared the richness of the natural surroundings, pink and blue layers of light over the lake as the sun vanished, leaving its optical mark. Another day was done, forest and its inhabitants resting until dawn of day, this day I awaken to, activity and light and, for me in the forest, always healing.

⁂

"The temptation is always to reduce life to size. A bowl of cherries. A rat race. Amino acids. Even to call it a mystery smacks of reductionism. It is the mystery. As far as anybody seems to know, the vast majority of things in the universe do not have whatever life is. Sticks, stones, stars, space—they simply are. A few things are and are somehow aware of it. They have broken through into Something, or Something has broken through into them. Even a jellyfish, a butternut squash. They're in it with us. We're all in it together, or it in us. Life is it. Life is with."

—Frederick Buechner, 1926

MY LAKE: All is calm, not a wave on the lake. Wait. As I sit on the rock at the edge of the shore, a flying object comes dive-bombing toward me. It plops into the lake before it reaches me, a weeny-teeny bug, a variety I have enjoyed watching these past few days. They amuse me with their little white wings, a body that curves into a tail of sorts. I reach into the water to help it, but my fingers only cause ripples that push it out a bit more. I patiently wait for it to drift in, this time with a stick for him to crawl onto. I have decided it is a him. I watch his little feelers guide him along and his spindly legs, no more than a fine thread. I see and hear a fish surface, eating one of the bug's buddies that has gotten stuck on the water surface. "That could have been you, buddy!" Some manage to fly off after landing on the water. Survival of the fittest?

I watch the flies walking busily over the rock next to me, as if on a mission, like the bustling New York City streets I left behind this week. The busy bumblebee buzzes from flower to flower on its journey to gather pollen from the pink whatever-they-are's. The only sign of life activity other than this within my radius is the notes of classical music from my father's portable radio up at the cabin, ever so faint. This leaves a silence for the passing birds to sing in, the woodpeckers to peck in.

I look down between the rocks to see a sparkling bridge of fine threads, which a spider has created for its use. A little green worm with a lime filament travels toward and around the ground in a fashion that makes it look suspended in air. He swiftly approaches, then hits a blade of grass, causing him to curl up in a U, starting to spin rapidly. He waits patiently until the spinning slows so he can continue on. The crows are crowing. The water is so still that I can see pools of dark fish, obviously breakfasting on my bug buddy's relatives—aunts, uncles, cousins. What a vast world is theirs, not unlike the city, the Big Apple.

Tiny bugs that glide on top of the water slide by remarkably quick, rippling the water as they make their way to their destination, or destiny, should a friendly fish come along. Like our life, theirs is a series of actions, reactions, and challenges meeting one's destiny or death along the way.

■ August 12, 1989: Remembering the Route that Got Us Here

[Notes above from this same Maine cabin, dut-dut* house, trip.]

*what my brother at age 2 called the cabin as they hammered nails, making a sound he described as "dut dut"

This summer we are taking the vacation together to our family cabin as we have been since my childhood; I am now thirty-four. Mom swooped us up every summer, leaving my father working in the jungle of the city, where he relished his work as a chemist, as well as his volunteer work with the Stamford Forum for World Affairs, world affairs and politics an interest of both of my community minded parents. Going back to this place has a special significance for us all, those days of childhood are more than a decade, almost two decades, past.

My parents say my brother was not sure if he could make the trip. Everything frightens him, even the prospect of a two-day leisure trip in a car, one of his favorite creations, one of his favorite destinations to what we consider paradise, to tranquility. He says he always remembers childhood as the best part of his life. I felt a twinge in my solar plexus, feeling deeply touched, when my parents said he decided to go when he found out I was going, too. I called him the night before departure to let him know I cared, to reinforce his joining us.

We start at 10 a.m., stopping at Howard Johnson's for lunch, which is when it started. My brother shifts into the other person, an anxious child in a grown man's forty-year-old body. Would we take him home? Would we take him to a hospital? He was in intense pain. His anxiety soars, unable to listen to reason or rationality. His ranting ramble continues. The words of the family doctor who predicted my emotional issues ring in my ears: "Everyone is a little schizophrenic."

I take him outside, suggest he breathe deeply, rubbing his chest with loving comfort (perhaps the comfort we did not get as infants?). His vocal cords tighten, he whines in a high squeaky voice, with fake tears trying to appear. I know his fears are just below all the tightness. He cannot drop down to where the real feelings are. My hope would be that with faith we can grab at those fears, pull them out and out. Miraculously, he calms down. We go back into the restaurant. People are staring at us. I smile and sit down.

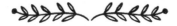

The mediocre teacher tells.
The good teacher explains.
The superior teacher demonstrates.
The great teacher inspires.

—William Arthur Ward

■ The True Change Begins

In 1987, Yogi Bhajan was in New York City for one of the many classes I would take from him there, in New Mexico at Solstice, and in the Millis, Massachusetts, ashram. My teacher, Ravi, said I needed a spiritual name. He proceeded to take me up to see Yogi Bhajan. Wearing green spandex leggings, hair chopped-short platinum from the job for a hair magazine I had recently taken out of necessity, I looked the epitome of the hip East Village artist. Yogi Bhajan stared at me with those intense eyes, asked my birthdate, wrote it on a tiny scrap of paper, the names based on numerology. He then said to me "Amrita Kaur, Princess of the Nectar of God, very special name."

Amrita is the elixir of immortality; the nectar is sweet and nourishing. It is said to be produced by stirring up the demons. Your spiritual name represents the journey of who you are. The more you repeat it, the stronger your directed destiny becomes.

In 1989, I attended my first Kundalini yoga summer solstice in the Jemez mountains of New Mexico, an annual gathering of one thousand or more yogis on the sacred lands of Yogi Bhajan's organization, where you feel the Native American presence of the past as you do in northern Maine. Ravi urged me to go but I was only able to attend because of a gift from a private client. Her card with a mandala on the cover said this:

Dear Donna,

Over these past few weeks, I've heard in your voice a tension that I used to know very well. [This woman was a singer who married an investment banker, even suggested funding a yoga studio for me, something I was not comfortable with, ready for, or felt deserving of.] I am enclosing this check so that perhaps a little bit of the pressure will be relieved. You may consider it a loan, a gift, whatever makes you most comfortable. Repayment is not important to me. What you've introduced to me has been invaluable on so many levels. I only hope that someday I'm able to do the same for you.

With love, affection, and admiration.
Lisa

The envelope and card contained a check for $500. I never repaid Lisa, who slipped out of my life, always to be remembered for her generosity and for the generosity of spirit that student's felt when I shared Yogi Bhajan's teachings.

Lisa buys me a small green tent and a sheepskin, which is what we sit on to practice Kundalini yoga. Her financial gift enables me to get to New Mexico. It is the first of ten consecutive and transformative ten-day summer solstice retreats in the dessert on land owned by Yogi Bhajan's organization, 3HO—Healthy, Happy, Holy. Eight miles up a dirt road outside a funky town, the site enveloped by the Jemez Mountains. We awake at 3:30 a.m. to meditate before the light appears, in the cool desert morning hours, feeling and watching the daylight arrive as we chant, moving in our sleepy bodies, a technique said to clear the subconscious; three days of partner meditation also a part of the cleansing process.

Various research being conducted so far confirms that there are certain periods in the night, between the hours of one and four in the morning, where chemicals are released in the brain that bring about feelings of connectedness to one's higher source. (a speculated reason is the darkness affecting the brain and its secretions)

That first solstice, I write Yogi Bhajan a note, dropping it in the box on the front stage, saying I am not personally or professionally happy. I receive a letter from him. The letter contains the meditation below, suggesting that I do it for eleven minutes for ninety days. I inhale before each thought, then let the breath and thought out with the *Wahe Guru*, the mantra for ecstasy, meaning going from the darkness to the light.

MEDITATION—
FOR REMOVING HAUNTING THOUGHTS

Center yourself with three deep inhalations and exhalations (or by chanting *Ong Namo Guru Dev Namo*).

Posture: Sit in any meditative posture, i.e., Easy Pose or in a chair with a straight spine with a light neck lock (Jalandhar Bandh).

Focus: Lower the eyelids until the eyes are only open 1/10th. Focus on the tip of the nose.

1. Silently say "*Wahe Guru*" in the following manner:
   Wha – mentally focus on the right eye.
   Hay – mentally focus on the left eye.
   Guru – mentally focus on the tip of the nose.

2. Remember the encounter or incident which happened to you. Mentally say "*Wahe Guru*" again in the above manner.

3. Visualize and personify the actual feeling of the encounter. Again, repeat "*Wahe Guru*."

4. Reverse roles in the encounter you are remembering. Become the other person and experience that perspective. Repeat "*Wahe Guru*."

5. Forgive the other person and forgive yourself.
   Repeat "*Wahe Guru.*"

6. Let go of the incident and release it into the Universe.
   Breath: Will come naturally.

Mantra: The mantra, "*Wahe Guru*," means "the indescribable joy of going from darkness to light."

Mudra: None specified.

Time: This can be done in 40 seconds!

End: Not specified.

Comments: This meditation can reduce phobias, fears, and neuroses. It can remove unsettling thoughts from the past that surface into the present, and it can take difficult situations in the present and release them into the hands of Infinity.

In 1999, ten years after that first summer solstice (I also attended five of the winter solstices in the early 1990s), I had a healing session with Guru Dev (who became renowned in Kundalini yoga circles), which he offered from his tent. He was a healer from Mexico who had developed a technique called Sat Nam Rasayan. Using this technique, he laid a few fingers on you while you were lying down, then made abstract comments (like your "coconut," or head, is better) or concrete suggestions, though not with an explanation why, like the meditation he gave me to do for ninety days, which had several steps, including flicking the tongue for twenty-two minutes. The tongue is significant for diagnosis in Ayurveda, a form of Eastern medicine. Placing the tip of the tongue to the roof of the mouth affects brain via meridians, energy points, in the palate. Guru Dev the healer suggests I eat lentils for eight weeks, only allowing raisins, eggplant, and P fruits in addition; I diligently did it, with no explanation as to why I was doing it. It was hard to refuse a piece of the raspberry pie my cousin Sam baked while I was in Maine with my family that summer. I lost a pound a week, getting thinner not the goal, but rather a discipline of the mind, the most important benefit of yoga. All my students said I looked amazing and radiant. Instead of caffeine, I drank Yogi Tea detox tea: One of the companies that Yogi Bhajan had started was the now world-famous Yogi Tea company. I had no idea if these things would heal or enlighten me. I believed strongly enough that it was worth a try.

Yogi Bhajan gave us seven steps to happiness. The first step was something I had run far away from in 1982, rationalizing an irrational commitment to something new. These yoga practices were bringing me back to the process that started with **Commitment.** Alyce, our house manager and a student from NYC, had come twice to the Sewall House (summer '98 and winter 2000) as a guest before joyfully helping us in 2002 as house manager. She sent me a card with this saying by Yogi Bhajan on it. "You should make yourself so happy, that by looking at you, other people become happy."

Despite my doubts and challenges, it was heartwarming to know the practice seemed to be working on some level when Alyce wrote that this quote reminded her of me.

Yogi Bhajan taught that we need not bring our garbage to others with complaining, that a compliment is always better. No one wants to see your toilet in their living room! He offers these seven steps to happiness:

1. Commitment. In every life, you are meant to commit. That is why the word is commit-*meant.* Commitment gives you **character.**

2. Character. Character is when all your characteristics—all facets, flaws, and facts—are under your control. Yin and yang meet there, totally balanced. Character gives you **dignity.**

3. Dignity. People start trusting you, liking you, respecting you. Dignity will give you **divinity.**

4. Divinity. Divinity is when people have no duality about you. They trust you right away. They have no fear about you. Divinity gives you **grace.**

5. Grace. Where there is grace, there is no interference, no gap between two people, no hidden agenda. Grace gives you the power to **sacrifice**.

6. Sacrifice. You can stand in any pain for that person. That sacrifice gives you **happiness**.

7. Happiness.

Yogi Bhajan predicted in the 1970's that the technology information age will be challenging because of rapid change, information overload; many people will experience mental and emotional challenges, evidenced today by high levels of anxiety, depression, and addiction. He believes Kundalini yoga can help these challenges, as do I.

Yogi Bhajan also gave five sutras, or "threads," to help us through this time, which he said would come to fruition in 2012. Kundalini yoga practice prepares us to meet these challenges.

The Five Sutras of the Aquarian Age

1. Recognize that the other person is you.

2. There is a way through every block.

3. When the time is on you, start, and the pressure will be off.

4. Understand through compassion or you will misunderstand the times.

5. Vibrate the cosmos, and the cosmos shall clear the path.

I avidly embraced Yogi Bhajan's teachings, being in his presence whenever possible—in New Mexico in June, Florida in December, and on the east coast whenever he visits, before he passes in 2004. I spend many hours at the feet of the Master, absorbing his wealth of wisdom.

Chapter 15

THE Z CHAPTER

At age thirty-three, in 1988, I jump on the opportunity to be in Maine for the summer. Stephen King is shooting the film version of his book *Pet Sematary*. I discover, via the producer who knew my business boyfriend beau Jeff through show business they both worked in, that they need a stand-in for the leading lady, Denise Crosby. I send in my headshot and land the job for $75 a day—yay! (Or was it $50?) I attended an acting summer school in New York City five days a week before *Pet Sematary*. My favorite Neighborhood Playhouse acting teacher, Richard Pinter, had suggested that we read Tolstoy, so with paperback edition of *War and Peace*, my bike for jaunts in Acadia National Park on days off, and my parents' old blue station wagon, I am off to Maine.

War and Peace is a good thing to have for the endless hours of sitting around, some all-night shoots at the airport, one all-night shoot on a field burning down a house. I make friends with the crew, mostly guys from LA, but also the casting director, Sue (who told me my brain would turn to Jell-O if I did too much yoga). My brain is more like Jell-O from the parties on the weekends. I develop a crush on the assistant director, a tall guy with very long dark hair, who shows up at a few of the parties. (He visited me once after the film, in my New York City apartment, pretty spooky at the time, the belongings of the Italian woman who had lived there for fifty years still there, old furniture and Madonna statues. The apartment had the haunting feeling of someone recently departed.) My name is in the credits at the end of the film's "special thanks" section. I barely knew this man, other than one fun night at the end of the film. He invited me to dinner. I spend the night. He still lingers in my mind.

Yogi Bhajan taught many lessons I slowly incorporate into my own life lessons, though not without trail (I meant *trial*, but sometimes dyslexia serves us) and error. One thing he says is, "If someone comes in the room and you feel your juices flowing, it is just your glands working—walk the other way. This was not love, only an exchange of bacteria!" (Yogi Bhajan, a customs official with a vast knowledge of yoga, had come to the United States in 1969 to get young people high on the *breath* rather than the drugs and sex that were so much a part of the hippie generation of the flower children he saw pouring into India in search of enlightenment. Addicts, he said, were looking for God in all the wrong places.)

Between sexualizing my feelings and being a passionate person who wanted to experience life, to break out from my past and experience the excitement of life—from the motorcycle I took my first honeymoon on to jumping out of airplanes—I often thrilled to seduction, masking my defensive heart which further deepened my emotional confusion. Pain and pleasure are opposite ends of the same spectrum, my yogi said. He taught that flirting was degrading to a woman. I had learned well how to flirt with my eyes, to speak what I thought was sexy. I took Yogi Bhajan's words to heart, studied his lectures. He said women were eagles, not "chicks." A woman's strength is in her grace and nobility, not her sexuality. I gradually learn a new way of being a woman.

In 1991, three years after *Pet Semetary*, Z walks in the door at a small engagement party for a girl I am taking a Shakespeare class with. This lanky, long-haired, dark-eyed guy immediately reminds me of the assistant director from Pet Sematary, lingering fantasies ignited, the feeling of seduction sparked.

An unhealthy, exciting, extended, often fun, often painful, chapter of my life that would last on and off for eleven years begins that night. Z gives me a ride home from the party in his hippie van. I pull out the one-woman story I am working on about Mary, my Maine great-grandmother. Addiction comes in many forms, consuming your thoughts, affecting the rest of your life. Mine was an obsession, a distraction, diluting the two directions that were important at this point in my life: acting, where I was considering making a go of it in Los Angeles, and learning and teaching yoga. I had recently broken off with my older show biz businessman boyfriend, Jeff, who was kind, good, helped me with business contacts. He'd taken me on ski trips to Utah and sunny trips to St. Bart's. His desire for children and for me to convert to Judaism were what ended our otherwise wonderful relationship. Z was Jewish, too, a free spirit. Jeff, a wonderful part of my personal and spiritual growth for a year and a half, had been a step forward in my healing. With Z, I was taking at least two steps back.

Keeping up with this free-spirited Peter Pan pot addict was such a pull that somehow I saved enough money to spend a month in Guatemala with him (and another "woman friend" of his) instead of moving to Los Angeles to pursue acting. Drama existed around everything we did, my emotions pushing and pulling my heartstrings, my self-esteem sinking. I did everything I could to make the relationship something it was not, chasing him to Brazil for ten days while he was in South America for six months, camping through Alaska for three weeks with him in 1992, an amazing trip where we shared our love for nature and new experiences among glaciers and national parks. All the travel was not all bad, having it's enriching moments.

He was all over the place (actually, all over the world) as I had been for years after leaving the U.S. in 1982. I stay as focused as I can on yoga and acting while following him. Besides the critical way he speaks to me, he sleeps around—like with the woman who nurses him when he breaks his neck jumping into a pool with very little water while in South America. When I discover his infidelities, I react by turning to someone else myself. Despite these damaging behaviors, the path of yoga gradually leads me out of this once again destructive pit.

In 1999, the patterns in this relationship that were filled with emotional distress culminate with the removal of a bladder tumor, a benign growth I believe was caused by the constant turmoil that had resulted in nearly two years of off-again on-again urinary tract infections. I'd never experienced UTI's before this relationship, despite my years of active sexual life. Z comes over the day of the surgery to force sex with me. I know there is a better way to live—beyond the self-loathing of eating disorders; beyond rejecting good things in my life like my first husband and career; beyond sleeping with men that did not care about me or me about them (and often having a drink or a drug to do so); beyond looking for attention and love in all the wrong directions, especially with this misogynist. All the while, I am teaching, working hard at my yoga and acting, knowing that I must still be capable of the happiness others see in me.

As I have said often when I teach yoga, Rome was not built in a day.

Yoga cleanses mind, body, and emotions so that you become aware of, alert to, and replace destructive thoughts, words, and acts with those of construction for yourself and positive contribution to others. Through Yogi Bhajan's yoga teachings I share the same concepts and possibilities with others. Though the thousands of students I have taught have no idea of the depth of the demons I fight, which take years to overcome, I continue to grow, revealing other challenges, as the spiritual path does. When the sex, drugs, and self-abuse are given up once and for all, replaced by other challenges, I face these new challenges from a place of clarity, depth of true feeling, acceptance, along with the contentment that yoga practice has given me.

Repeatedly, I have rejected healthy, loving relationships as I continue my search for self-love, including the British man who I was seeing when I turned forty, a good solid man and a loving relationship, who wrote and sent me this to me on my fortieth birthday:

This day. Forty years ago, at approximately 4:30 p.m., Mrs. Harriett Miller gave birth to a beautiful baby daughter. Her name was Donna after her Uncle Don (although not too many people know that).

Donna has been down many paths and has had many experiences, some more beautiful and meaningful than others.

Eventually, she found the spiritual path and was given a spiritual name, Amrita, by a very incredible and wise man, Yogi Bhajan.

Donna grows more beautiful every day and is loved by many.

However, there is one individual with whom she made a spiritual connection on April 8, 1994, who loves her with all his heart.

With this fax, sent close to her birth time, he sends more birthday wishes to coincide with that spiritual moment in the cosmos:

Happy birthday to you, happy birthday to you, happy birthday, Dear Donna, happy birthday to you.

Some wise words from Yogi Bhajan:

Love is a sacrifice.

Love is not a projection; love is an attraction. Love is a sacrifice.

Love has no limit. When it has a limit, then it is not love.

When your doubts are gone, then your fears will be gone. Your feelings and experiences will be of happiness. Between two people there is a god; among three, a whole government.

Donna, I love you.

So powerful, his message. His love. His understanding of me, who I was, where I had been. Again, I rejected. Learning to receive love was not yet possible, ability to give love still developing. Once again, rejection of another. Self-contempt can only reject another. Hope carries the day: It is possible, but we cannot rush our own timing or what it can cause for the unfolding, the learning more about the true self, which is the ability to give and receive love from a place of purity. After rejecting this healthy man, Z came back in—more drama, but with it an idea he gave me that changed my life direction once again. Finally I would close the chapter with him.

■ January 6, 2009: A New Year, First Writing

Barry, a deep-baritone friend I had met through yoga was a bit on the eccentric side but nice, also attended Aunt Nancy's hundredth birthday party in 1995. Barry had become enthralled with my family history—and maybe with me, too. When it was Barry's turn to greet Aunt Nancy in her green leather chair by the window near the fireplace, Barry shook her hand, looked down, and exclaimed, "Wow, you still have great legs!" Aunt Nancy, a reserved, very sweet New Englander, was gracious, ignoring his comment. Paul, the funny and handsome Brit, (who wrote the 40th birthday message to me) one of the truly nicest guys I had been with since my first husband, brought Aunt Nancy a little book on Geronimo, knowing that Aunt Nancy loved to tell the story of meeting him when she was ten years old at TR's in-auguration. Telling her father that she would like to shake Geronimo's hand, her father (my great grandfather) had said, "If you want to do something, do it." His words gave her the courage to saunter up to Geronimo. When she shook his hand, it felt like a soft glove despite many battles. (Z would later violently tear out the page where Paul had written his inscription. I have not seen the book in years. Z often did contemptuously hurtful things, but on this celebratory day, I did not know any of these things to come: Z had left my life to marry a woman he'd met in Brazil. (Little did I know he would return).

Aunt Nancy joyfully gathered family and friends to celebrate her life of simplicity and love in the house she had been born in and would die in near her beloved Mattawamkeag Lake. If people spoke of beautiful parts of the world they had traveled, Aunt Nancy would say, "It doesn't have anything on Mattawamkeag." She knew the birds, the gardens, and the wildflowers well, having been educated by her father, the acclaimed nature guide.

When it came time to cut the cake, Aunt Nancy stood over the cake, singing along with the birthday song, exclaiming, "Happy Birthday to ME!" her old blue eyes glittering, the smile of a little girl splashed across her face, the same little girl whose father had told her ninety-five years before, "Nancy, this house is built on honor."

Yale Stevens, a local carpenter who had restored the barn, took videos of us all lined up on the front porch. A few years earlier, he had helped renovate my mom's cabin, then a few years later, he would take his own life after losing his wife and then his girlfriend to cancer. On this day, however, Yale was our gregarious videographer.

Little did I know (despite my staged reading of "In This, Our Home" in the same year as Aunt Nancy's party) that this would become "this, my home" within two years.

I was still femme fatale-ing around, flirting and looking for that happiness from external attention. Though I had now been practicing Kundalini yoga for ten years, residual parts of my old behaviors were still present, motivated by the wounds I had been working for so long to heal in many and strange ways—careers, relationships, travels. Working on it, maybe even sometimes understanding it. But I had further to go, including more of the Z chapter. My addiction to him yearned for the excitement of the ups and downs of passion, even the hurt he had wrought. I missed the drama of being with him despite the good in my life.

"Whenever you deploy yourself to make a man feel you and want you, the moment his want is satisfied, you will be in the garbage. You cannot change the law. After you finish eating from a plate of food, what do you do with it? Either you put it in the refrigerator as a left-over or you put it in the garbage. Do you think this, which is a normal law, does not apply to you? You started the sequence, you reaped the consequences, and still you want to blame someone else. That is your love life... Instead, present yourself to be sought after. Make yourself a caliber that is sought after. Somebody should seek you rather than desire you."

—Yogi Bhajan

Chapter 16
CARELESS CARETAKER

■ **Written November 2008**

A dear New York City friend (and fellow yoga teacher), Stephen, tells me about two things in 1999, Ashtanga yoga and the *Caretaker Gazette*. Guru Dev had suggested to me in a healing session with him in 1996 that I was a good teacher, but that to be great, I needed to be more physically integrated, which the physically challenging Ashtanga form would help with. (Guru Dev was the one who had also told me to eat lentils for eight weeks and do a meditation where I flicked my tongue like a snake for twenty minutes a day for ninety days, among other things.) My friend Stephen loans me an Ashtanga yoga video led by an Indian man named Patabhis Jois. Wearing only shorts, very different from the flowing robes that covered Yogi Bhajan's body, this older Indian gentleman guides half a dozen students through an impossible-looking Ashtanga yoga routine. Stephen tells me that one of the students on the tape, a red-haired young man named Eddie Stern, has become well-known in the Ashtanga yoga world, almost a "rock star" in a saturated market. This was my first foray into a completely different form of yoga than Kundalini, another branch of the yoga tree that would change my life and my yoga teaching. Ashtanga is very physically demanding, developed for healthy teenaged boys but having gained popularity for people of all ages. This leads me to study other forms of physically oriented yoga—Dharma Yoga, Iyengar, and to try additional forms of yoga as well.

The *Caretaker Gazette*, which Stephen thought also might be of use to me, is a publication offering caretaking positions, some paid, some not. In 2002, I found an impeccable chef (and person) for Sewall House through *Caretaker Gazette*. When the pipes almost froze in the winter of 1999, the thought of a caretaker seemed like a good one. On the day the pipes freeze I want to drive up in the morning from New York City. Z, who keeps crazy hours, suggests we drive all night to arrive for breakfast with my mother's cousin Bill, which means arriving around 5 a.m. With his charming way of pushing himself on people, Z has seemingly ingratiated himself to Bill, who has become, in Z's eyes, a surrogate grandfather. When Bill and I have a moment alone, Bill looks at me with those sparkling blue Sewall eyes, his strong body slowly succumbing to Parkinson's, saying "Are you all right?" with care, as if he knows I am in a bad situation, which I am. He says no more.

When we arrive at the house, the third-floor bathroom sink and kitchen sink faucets are beginning to freeze. We call the plumber, a friend of Bill's and Aunt Nancy's—Bob, an energetic little man, youthful beyond his years. He comes over immediately, using a hair dryer to warm the pipes. The following summer, the pipe on the third floor in the new bathroom leaks into the ceiling of the bathroom below it. The ice that day must have formed a crack that causes a leak the following summer when we have a house full of guests. (A guest came downstairs and said, "Do you know your second-floor bathroom ceiling is leaking water?" Another panic moment of looking for a worker to get to the issue.)

The house continues to teach me. Z had urged me to buy the house, saying it was ready to open its doors to the public. If I opened the house, he said people would come. Had I seen all that needed to be done—the old soft mattresses, the stained once beautiful wallpaper, the antiquated appliances, or the draft holes throughout the house—it certainly might have stopped me. What I saw was the potential of saving a legacy, part of which had already been taken from us when my great-grandfather's fantastic spot with its eight individual cabins had been sold out from under the family's nose. Keeping Sewall House breathing was our family's last chance to keep some of the legacy alive, the part/house TR had lived and breathed in amidst his healing jaunts in the nearby woods.

The first two winters (1997 and 1998) that I owned the house, Z lived there. I was in therapy, as per my acting manager's suggestion, telling my therapist that I resented Z living in the house while I paid all the bills from my (not high) yoga teaching salary. I took on a roommate in New York City to help pay the Sewall House bills. Z kept the house at a chilly 55 degrees, considerate, but made no offer to help financially. When our relationship evolved from bad to worse, my therapist would tell me he was a sociopath.

The memory of the feelings of that little girl sticking her toe in the water, smiling, laughing, saying "thum-day," not jumping because of fear, was renewed as I faced one fear after the other: Can I pay the (albeit relatively small) mortgage, oil, taxes, electricity, plowing, etc., etc.? Can I prove to my family, more importantly to myself, that I can do this?

One of my close friends in Paris, Ula, a Danish model, had said, "The universe always takes care of Donna." The other day when a young yoga teacher learned that I split my time between Maine and NYC, she said, "What a dream," and I responded, "I am in that dream", implying that no one knows what it takes to live our dreams, what we have gone through, what has worked for us, what hasn't, where we have sacrificed, where we have gained.

On a cold winter morning in Maine, one more lesson. Again, the universe had "taken care": The pipes had not totally frozen, which would have ruined the walls and the house.

Since no one was living in the house the winter the pipes froze, I decide to look for someone to live there for the following winter, 2000. I run an ad in the *Caretaker Gazette*, getting a response from a young man from New Jersey who lives off the grid. He has a sweet wife he met in Colorado when teaching martial arts. We speak on the phone, he sends a résumé, has been the caretaker/handyman of a museum. His only reference is from a relative (overlooked red flag). His interests and lifestyle appear to be a good match—nature, meditation, clean living, things dealing with spirit. Z interviews him, agreeing we all share a "common bond." The first winter, 2000, goes well. Sort of.

Z, who thinks of himself as my manager, has the brilliant idea to invite his friend, a pot-smoking buddy named Gary who he has met in his Brooklyn neighborhood, to drag his handyman equipment up from Brooklyn in his old station wagon, live in the garage, which is not insulated or heated, to do "projects" on the house.

The caretaker "White Wolf," the off-the-grid, nature-loving father and husband who has a young son, feels unsure about Gary, allowing him in the house only for bathroom and kitchen use. The house is still kept at 55 degrees, my request to help me manage the bills. The family does so without complaint. Though not warm, the house is definitely more comfortable than the subzero temperatures outside, where White Wolf often wandered for hours. Gary's first task is to create a "living space" in the garage corner. When I arrive for Christmas, Gary has torn out the existing stairs to the upper garage with plans to create a spiral staircase in a different spot than the original stairs. There's now a hole in the second floor of the garage corner which, if finished, might have been fantastic. He installs a woodstove made from a barrel, cutting a hole out the roof for a stovepipe. Gary insulates the walls in the little corner floor area. A wide-open second-floor space is above this, where the heat escapes to a mattress on the floor. The concept was good, the project never completed, perhaps a combination of the pot, cigarettes and lonely depression from the isolation. The family inside the house was not welcoming to him. I wondered if all the things he had torn out would jeopardize the house being on the National Register of Historic Places.

Seeing no progress, and concerned whether the project would be completed, I communicate with Gary, all the while paying him as agreed upon (not much but a stretch for me). I ask him to leave by February. He does, probably relieved. Gary, a harmless guy, is definitely not the ideal yoga retreat handyman.

The caretaker stays. Having lived all over the United States, his sweet wife with the squeaky little-girl voice had left her job as a chemist to follow him off into the woods. He wanders in the woods for hours. When Z and I split, he takes Z's side. The caretakers depart early their second winter, but not before cutting my great-grandfather's bearskin rug in half while also stealing a buffalo horn from the Theodore Roosevelt ranch. My great-grandfather had brought back the horn from his days living with TR in Medora, North Dakota, where he built TR's Elkhorn Ranch. My great grandfather lived in Medora for two years with TR in North Dakota before returning to Island Falls in the 1870s. I was devastated when I discovered they were gone. My mother had allowed them to spend the summer near her lake property after others complained of them living elsewhere (as squatters) on the lake. This is what I got in return. The first winter, we had gotten along well. When I visited at Christmas we had nice chats. They were gracious. When they left, they left behind a black mark from smoke on the ceiling above the fireplace, which became one of the motivations to clean up and upgrade the walls and ceilings. The fireplace heated the living room beyond the cool temperature the house was set at. The ceiling marks could be repaired. The violation of the cutting the heirloom bearskin rug and stealing the irreplaceable buffalo horn contradicted all the values this man seemed to present and be.

White Wolf had penned a self-published book about his lessons from a Native American man he claimed to have encountered in the woods of New Jersey (much like the well-known tracker Tom Brown). Some of our guests "bought" his story (as did I at the time), reading it with fascination. He was a modern-day Tarzan, with long hair, handsome features, and a fit body. Uncle Don and Cousin Sam (two of the men I bought the house from) read the story, taking it with a grain of salt. Sam, ever the non-judger, helped them whenever they needed something. These people were only one of the lessons I would learn along the way of the journey, my commitment to keep the Sewall House grounded, safe, and alive.

The repercussions from the caretakers' presence did not stop with their leaving. White Wolf sent me a letter after their quick departure (leaving food to rot in the refrigerator) telling me that the house had evil spirits from the yoga retreat guests. Kent, who came to Sewall House in 2001 as one of my yoga students offering to help, eventually becoming my next husband in 2003, suggested it was *their* energies, and Z's energy, that needed to be cleared.

The clearing continued. First, Kent painted the exterior of the house; next came the interior, the two of us wallpapering and working intensely together on the internal house (a metaphor perhaps?) in 2003, the winter before we got married. Sorting through the contents Aunt Nancy had left behind, the years of my family history held within these walls, was continuing the excavation inside myself that had started when I left my first marriage, life chiseling away.

Some days I wondered if White Wolf was lurking in the woods. Kent looked him up on the Internet, finding that he was teaching his outdoor living techniques in the woods of Vermont. I googled White Wolf today, twelve years later, and found only images of a stunning beast; a white wolf truly is a beautiful creature. Though it might not seem related, I would see a white wolf live on stage in April 2015 at the Stamford Symphony, bringing my white wolf experience to a beautiful full circle: Helene Grimaud, a wolf hero and gifted pianist whom I discovered that day, would motivate me to become active in wolf conservation.[3]

---

[3] Learn more at http://nywolf.org. The beautiful wolf Atka died in Sept 2018, see https://nywolf.org/ambassador-wolves/atka.

Chapter 17
COMING HOME

"Yoga makes our life become more clear, more conscious, not more easy, but more aware, alive and alert."

—Donna Amrita Davidge

Today a student told me that her yoga practice makes her feel she has come home. Tears were in her eyes.

In 1997, the year I purchased Sewall House, it held all the ramifications of "coming home." What I didn't see was what had to be done to the home. What I saw instead was the mysterious magic that the house represented to me as a child, the rooms so rarely glimpsed, full of treasures and curiosities. These rooms were now mine to freely view. I failed to take in the faded wallpapers, the water stains, the deep layers of muck on the kitchen linoleum, hidden from view under the radiators, the soft un-sleep-able mattresses.

I had two groups of "guests" the first season: the first a group of curious yoga students, the other formed by a yoga friend who had attended Aunt Nancy's 100th birthday with me (Barry, one of *three* men who accompanied this wild forty-year-old child). The latter group came out of curiosity for the historic home's connection with TR. The group included Barry, a male friend of his, the friend's eighty-five-year-old mother, his girlfriend, and her twenty-six-year-old daughter. This odd yoga group explored the "unorganized territory" of Sewall House. No yoga studio existed yet. The parlor space used for weddings and funerals was a good space to do yoga since it was clear of furniture. The parlor also provided the room to put the eighty-five-year-old in a chair for yoga.

The attached shed became the yoga studio once the many layers of clutter it contained were removed. The shed was filled wall to wall with canning jars, barrels full of odds and ends, from glassware to Easter grass, as well as the filth that accompanies years of accumulation in spaces that invite it. This shed, which originally held ten cords of wood to get through harsh winters in a drafty home, was poorly insulated with newspapers and horsehair. With its pantry full of pie tins and other supplies for Aunt Nancy's busy kitchen, the shed was gradually transformed into the yoga studio. Being right off the kitchen, the "yoga" shed was conveniently located. The first transformation of the attached shed occurred in 1999. The space had been cleared and cleaned several times, with raw wood floors, dingy wood-paneled walls (wide panels of wood from the huge trees they cut in those days that were no more). Carpet scraps from Walmart were the first yoga/meditation pads. With $2500 from my meager (but helpful!) settlement after being hit by a cab in New York City the same year I bought the house, insulation, drywall, and paneling happened. The pantry was converted to a sauna, first with a used sauna element. A propane heater hung on the wall to heat the yoga space, which was drafty from the shed doors that would be replaced with French doors and a beautiful wood burning style propane stove as the transformation continued.

Little by little, the yoga space and the house welcomed refreshing touches—healing touches—some minor, some major. We worked every winter and spring break while my husband Kent, who had first come to Sewall House as a volunteer work-study in 2001, was at City College NY getting his music degree, to empty each bedroom, one at a time, into the hallway so that we could wallpaper. Kent painted the ceilings, wide wood floors, and windows. Since the house had been on the National Register of Historic Places since 1970, the heavy wooden windows, as well as the wood exterior, were required to stay. Kent's mother, Inga, came from Sweden to help in winter 2003. I learned to be part of a wallpapering team. Kent and I continued wallpapering rooms when Inga was not here to help. With Kent on board lovingly restoring the house, the house responded, breathing as Kent did things like lift linoleum floors to reveal original wood—the spirits happier, the house energy flowing more alive. Kent worked hard.

Kent's first project was painting the exterior of Sewall House during his work-study in the summer of 2001, using cheap paint from Walmart, all I could afford at the time. The internal work on the house began over Kent's college breaks after we became a couple, starting with the month before our wedding in the backyard in 2003. In that month, he and his mother, back again to help, wallpapered the living room. Kent painted on the wall *Donna and Kent, married 2003* for any person in the future who might peel the many layers of living off the walls as we had done, discovering beautiful old wallpapers layered over each other. The house was like the yoga practice, peeling away the physical layers, feeling under that the layers of life, the emotion, the love and work and play that had occurred within these walls since 1865. Creating home.

The kitchen had been upgraded by Aunt Nancy in 1945. Materials at that time were hard to find because of World War II. She reworked the existing kitchen, creating a big, wide-open kitchen, with counters built by Bill Sewall and cupboards built by her nephew Sam using uneven-sized wood. Sam explained that un-matched wood was all they had to work with because of the war. Off the kitchen on the first floor was the garage to the east, where the sun rose, beautifully greeting the porch each day.

The front of the house had at one point had a large door in the dining room facing east. That space was now two large windows letting in morning light though we preferred to experience the morning sun sitting on the wraparound porch outside these welcoming windows. Kent and I got to know each other sipping morning coffee as the sun rose that first summer of 2001 while guests slept. The quiet young man from Sweden and the talkative high-energy yoga teacher he had met on one of his first days in the country, wondering that day if all American women talked so much.

Through the dining room and forward is the living room with the original fireplace, where we have added a woodstove with a glass window for heat efficiency, a nook turned into a popular window seat by Sam after I bought the house. The extraneous chairs in the living room were removed to the third-floor "library," as is any family photo, old book, or artifact that requires exile from the publicly used rooms and private bedrooms. We reupholstered the green living room sofa and its matching chair with a mustard-colored fabric found in the New York City textile district on sale, to be reworked by our growing cat family. To the north of the living room is the hallway connecting back to the dining room through one of the many doors in the house; another such door is an undersized one in the "Pine-cone Room," so named for its wallpaper with large fluffy pinecones, a paper that had once been bright white. The wallpaper had become the consistency of chalk. Once a beautiful and unique wallpaper, this one was the most difficult for me to relinquish. I found a beige paper with tiny pinecones, but, unhappy with losing the fluffy large pine-cones, I settled on a regal rich green pattern, like the pine forest, and gold, like the sunlight, from England on sale at Sherwin-Williams, as were all the wallpapers.

The first wallpaper we purchased was for use in the downstairs bedroom, once my great-grandfather's study, where Uncle Maurice's pipe collection, which had been hanging on the wall along with his rifle rack, had since been removed. The gun rack was removed, rele-gated to the "library" on the third floor, only one rifle and one pistol left. The pistol had etchings of the Nina, Pinta and Santa Maria, which a guest years later told me was likely of some value. Knowing nothing about it, I gathered this had been one of the many gifts TR had sent my great grandfather over the years as he requested maple candy and hand woven wool socks in return. The pipe rack and pipes long gone with the many things I chose to discard, always wondering if I was discarding some family treasure, or junk, or something the *Antiques Road Show* might have told me had value. Some things just disappeared amongst so much stuff I could not keep track of with no time to create an inventory of it all.

Between the dining room and downstairs office (turned into a bedroom for Aunt Nancy in her senior years; now a bedroom for guests) was a sturdy safe with large, richly colored pink roses painted on the inner door, discovered once you could get the combination to magically open it. This house I called beautiful, Aunt Nancy insisted was "rugged". Perhaps *rugged* is a more useful trait in life, as well as for a house. The safe contained only a few odds and ends—the handwritten will of Levi Sewall, my great-great-grandfather who founded Island Falls in 1845; a wooden ring with a coin ornament, sent from an imprisoned Indian during the Civil War; baby pins and rings. A curious set of stairs stands behind the safe, leading to the second-floor bathroom, perhaps an interim stairway in the five years of building the house before the formal cherry-wood bannister spiraled up the three layers of the house, perhaps simply a convenient passageway to preserve heat rather than going to the formal front staircase. These are the kinds of questions I asked myself, wishing there was someone to answer them instead of the imaginary conversation with my great-grandmother in "In This, Our Home." I would have asked her the questions of life my childhood poem "Why" still posed, imagining somehow that her pioneer existence might have answered some of my contemporary questions about life and happiness.

The downstairs bedroom, where Aunt Nancy was found dead on the floor on January 8, 1996 (a day on which New York City was blanketed in snow with everything shut down), now contained the energy from the careless caretakers who had occupied it. Wallpapering this room first seemed a good beginning to refresh the energy. When my mother passed in 2004, (same year Yogi Bhajan died) the $3000 she leaves me is the exact amount needed for adding a small shower in the closet of the half bath in this room, creating the first full-bath bedroom, which I anoint the "Sewall Suite." Kent thought this was false advertising, as the room is not huge like a suite, the bathroom tiny; I chose the name because it was alliterative, alluding to the fact that this guest bedroom room had a full bath.

Wooden signs for each room were made by a man from Sweden, all the way to the third floor, where the two smaller bedrooms became Wilbur and Harriett, named for my mom and dad. The Wilbur room, already paneled by Uncle Maurice, had a masculine feeling. The Harriett room, with the curved ceiling cascading horsehair insulation when I bought the house, was transformed into a dainty feminine room by an Australian traveler I met on the train en route to Maine in 1999. He visited for a few days in exchange for paneling the room. He owned a hostel in Australia and had done all the carpentry there himself. He suggested I buy other houses nearby to expand my vision. The Sewall House was enough of an undertaking by itself, financially and otherwise, for a yoga teacher living on a fluctuating uncertain income.

Gradually the house revives with love, attention, infusions from different directions. Across from the third-floor bedrooms (where cousin Sam had lived as a child, he and brother Gene in one bedroom, his parents, Merrill, one of my great grandfather's 5 children, and Myrtle, in the other) is now the "library." This was once the dining-living and kitchen rooms for Uncle Merrill (one of my great-grandparents' five children) and his wife, Aunt Myrkie, the ones who would later run the Sewall Camps on the lake. The library becomes the room for any and all historic things related to family that might spook a guest. Andrew Vietze's book on the friendship between my great-grandfather and TR ("Becoming Teddy Roosevelt How a Maine Guide Inspired America's 26th President", published 2010, Down East books, nominated for an independent publishing award) says the third floor "library" room is a tribute to Theodore, as Aunt Nancy always called him. There are books about TR, copies of fast-fading fax-paper letters from TR to my great-grandfather (which had been sold to the Harvard Library), as well as many other family artifacts not related to TR: tiny children's black and white leather shoes, the original post office (a handmade tall wooden box with separate compartments inside for the mail of the pioneer population of Island Falls), my great-grandfather's handcrafted wooden baby rocking bed, to name a few. The library is also home to my favorite thing in the house, the thing I would have claimed when we were told we could each take one thing before the contents were auctioned. Originally hanging in the now "Sewall Suite", it is a large framed painting of a seven-year-old Aunt Nancy in winter hat, coat, and muffs. She's holding a fluffy black-and-white cat that looks like a combination of our two fluffy cats and the tiny black-and-white one who all came on board after I buy the house.

An early (2000) retreat guest wanted to buy my great-grandfather's leather rocking chair (where, I was told, he would sit for hours reading those letters from TR in front of the living room fireplace but is now also in the third floor library, showing its age). I kept the chair. I do sell Aunt Nancy's plentiful costume jewelry to early guests as we clear out the house. One young woman actually came strutting downstairs in a dress that had been hanging in Aunt Nancy's closet. She asks if she can keep the dress. (The house was still not prepared for the general public, as evidenced by dresses hanging in the closet.) I let her keep it! The process of clearing and cleaning over 130 years of history, the everyday stuff of living, some things junk, other things precious memories and gems of another time, was magical and mysterious, like the house. It is a lot, this house. (The house now 150 years old as I finish this story 22 years after buying it).

I recall the day Uncle Don dropped me off in the driveway, saying in his matter-of-fact, unanimated, slow-paced northern Maine accent, "I hope this house never becomes a burden." Whether or not it will, I have to try, to see if I can keep it going, this house built on honor. Aunt Nancy had kept the tradition going. It seems someone else should now.

The third floor houses a dark walk-in closet under the rafters with books from Sam's school days, his childlike signature on the inside of the front covers, old bullets stored on the shelves. This was the perfect place to put the first additional bathroom, done in 1998 for $10,000. Like a squirrel, I hoarded cash from private clients and from the yoga center (before they attended the Zen business boot camp and slashed my pay). From my parents and the habit of living on little or nothing from my modeling and acting days, I have learned to be excessively frugal. My accountant in the city says I have survived by "eating ramen", a metaphor for frugality paying off.

(In 1985, when I first arrived in New York City, I often subsisted on a $1.25 large bran muffin, making that last the day, walking eight miles some days in the winter on modeling go-sees that led to no jobs. Anorexia now a long-gone thing from my past, my first days in NY I look back on as necessity starvation in my efforts to not give up, to keep pushing the dream as I had done in Europe.)

The second floor has four bedrooms, each with its own theme, unoccupied for years except the front east bedroom, which receives the morning sun, the room where Aunt Nancy and Uncle Maurice had slept when young and able, where my great-grandparents slept before them.

Room by room, whenever Kent has a break from City College, we are in Maine to work nonstop, emptying out each room, wallpapering, discovering with wonder all the styles and layers of wallpaper that had gone before. Kent paints the ceilings and windowsills. Bit by bit with the on-sale Sherwin-Williams wallpaper, we manage to complete each room, replacing the soft mattresses one by one, as well.

Like the student who said yoga felt like coming home, this rooting back into the family home is my way to commit to a home, a concept I had rejected for so many years by chasing around the planet after losing my home in San Diego.

Chapter 18
STAFF

■ **Staff Starts at Sewall House Yoga Retreat, 2000
(written August 24, 2008)**

Before I knew we would be featured that season in *InStyle* magazine, I decided we needed a staff, starting with a chef. With such public exposure, the house was not ready for the bookings that came pouring in through the magazine, though my mate at the time, Z, convinced me it was ready. In overalls, I sat in the kitchen with an electric cord stretching across the floor to plug in my used Dell laptop, my makeshift desk in the "nook" of the kitchen, the same nook where my great-grandfather's sister Sarah sat sorting the mail. The house was the first post office in Island Falls, evidenced by the covered over slot in the original heavy wood door in the kitchen near the nook.

Our first chef, Louisa, the quirky, beautiful vegan who had responded to our job listing on a yoga studio wall, prepared me a delicious meal in NYC as an interview, including chocolate mousse made with tofu. When she arrived at Sewall House her meals were not the same as the first one she offered in the city. She also said she did not want to make desserts. She slept in a small room above the kitchen, which I thought was convenient but spooked her. It was next to my room which was also dark and unfinished. While my bedroom was actually the upper shed (like a cabin to me, who luxuriated in its size of a NYC loft), hers had been used as a bedroom in the "olden days" for relatives who were not renters but needed a place to stay.

After a month of enjoying Louisa's company, wishing her food were as good as the meal she had prepared for me on her interview, I was on the phone in the window seat in the living room talking with the woman who owned the New York City studio that I was affiliated with at the time, Kundalini Yoga East. She had called to ask how things were going. I was reporting how great things were going as I looked out the window. I spotted Louisa struggling with two huge suitcases as she dragged them across the front lawn. There is no public transport in Island Falls, just one bus south at 9 a.m. via the town of Sherman ten miles to the south. She left without a word of explanation. I suspect it was discomfort with Z, who could be controlling towards her in the kitchen, despite it now being her domain, as well as with his friend Gary, whom she had told me made her feel uncomfortable. Her odd bedroom likely did not help her experience either.

My stomach dropped as I saw her depart, the panic of how we would now feed the guests. The massage therapist and Z unexpectedly stepped into the kitchen. The problem was quickly solved, but not my feelings of hurt and misunderstanding about why she walked out with no notice. A few years later, Louisa popped up in a packed class I was subbing for my teacher, Ravi Singh (Sewall House had been her introduction to Kundalini yoga), acting as if I were a long-lost friend. She was working in a vegan restaurant and said I should check it out. Needless to say, I never got there as I was still holding onto the uncomfortable feelings brought on by her quick departure

Fast-forward to March 2011. I have not of late subscribed to *Yoga Journal*, but my dear old ninety-six-year-old-dad has done it for me. There is an article on chefs. There, in front of me on the page, is Louisa, smiling up at me. She has a book published by Random House, starting the article by saying that a summer spent cooking at a yoga retreat in Maine in exchange for room and board jump-started her career. I look her up on Facebook, send her an e-mail; she writes back saying she is getting married in April, that her walking out on me had been reactive, that I had been right when I told her she was reactive. I don't remember telling her that. I do remember that the difference between responding and reacting is one of the first and biggest lessons that I learned from Yogi Bhajan: be a responder, not a reactor. So much of my own life has been a reaction—to pain, to insecurity. Despite the reaction I felt inside me when she left Sewall House that day, I had stayed neutral and nonreactive when she showed up in that class in New York City, a result of my practice.

My close friend Denyse said to me recently, "You were not so worried about money when you were younger." The truth is I was terrified of growing old with no money, even when I was married to Ron, where money would never be an issue, and despite my flourishing nutrition career at the time. I remember attending workshops on mutual funds (for dietitians) and telling Ron we had to start investing; I was irrationally afraid. The feeling seemed rooted from the first time I stuck the big toe in the water and did not jump in; from other times kicking behind the locked attic door; from hearing the word *ignore* (what my mother spelled out to others when I was young and acting out to get attention) when I was so young I didn't know what I-G-N-O-R-E meant. When the fear and anxiety feelings welled up, I turned to another man, maybe a drink to loosen me up, anything to fill the void. With the control issues of anorexia still embedded, I also controlled my intake of drugs or alcohol, never leading to addiction, though my behaviors with men, especially the abusive one in my forties, demonstrated a pattern of reaction, turning away from my own fears and feelings by replacing them with impulsive excitement.

I told Louisa when I saw her that I too was working on applying in my life the principles of not reacting to one's own fear with destructive behaviors, making sure that the constructive behaviors did not become another form of addiction. When we could truly listen to our inner voice, make our own decisions for harmony and balance, we would not need to have some guru tell us to rise at 3 a.m. every day, exhausted but now, ah, supposedly more spiritual because of it. Tools like early morning meditation can help us break the patterns of the mind but also exhaust us. In the end we need to find and utilize the tools that work for us and apply them often. In yoga breathing, chanting and poses are those tools.

I had my own challenges with Z and Gary present at Sewall House that summer. Louisa said that she had not seen that. Having the bad beau Z (a form of addiction) and his handyman friend, both potheads, at this healing haven was something I had not yet found the strength to weave out. That summer, however, Z saved the mission, stepping into the kitchen with the massage therapist, a talented and fun girl from New York City that a friend had referred to us. The retreat survived another season. One more (of many to come) Sewall House dilemmas solved.

I was gratified that Louisa had used the experience as a jumping-off point for success. Sewall House had once again served another.

It was not until winter 2015, fifteen years later, that the issue of her walking out in 2000 felt finally resolved. I ran into Louisa on the street a few blocks from my New York City apartment the day after I returned from Maine in October 2014. As we spoke, she told me that she studied yoga with a young woman who had come to chef for a week at Sewall House that summer. (I had never met the woman who had cooked that season for us until she came highly recommended by one of my students who was her best friend.) Louisa mentioned that she was going to be offering tastings on Monday evenings for the month of December at a small restaurant in the East Village; it had been featured in either *New York Magazine* or the *New Yorker.* Things kept getting in the way of my getting there, but finally I did, inviting my dear friend Denyse to join me. (Denyse had been the stage manager in a play I was in, and we had become fast friends twenty years before. She had caught the bouquet at my 2003 wedding. She passed away in July 2016 as a result of the unhealthy living that sadness can cause.) We tasted whatever I could with my vegetarian palate, including a luscious pistachio ice cream creation. The bill was not going to be small. Louisa would float out to speak with the various customers who lined up at a long table in a small space. She was as sweet as when I met her, telling us about her musician husband and her plans to make an Iranian cookbook based on her roots. When the bill arrived, she sauntered out, picked it up, looked me in the eye and said, "I think we are even now, Donna," acknowledging that she had taken something away that summer. Now she had given back. I was touched. Patience pays; another lesson from Yogi Bhajan. (the complete version of his words on patience is at the end of this book).

■ Staff Continues at Sewall House, 2001— it gets even crazier (written September 4, 2008)

The air is amazing. The sun so beautifully strong. The fog lifting gracefully off the lake. Exhaustion from working nonstop 5:30 a.m. to 10:30 p.m. for over a month; before that, a ten-day break, but still doing things as a house, a business, and people require. It has been our best season to date.

The last fall that I had any appreciable time here was 2001, the fall of 9/11. Glad to be out of New York City that fall, for sure.

Processing all that had gone down that summer as I kept the business going while dealing with strange turmoil of Z exiting, Kent entering.

Jeff and Christina, a young couple from Florida, served as both cooks and massage therapists that summer. They insisted on silence in the kitchen while they made delicious vegan food. We started the season with Olivia, a young "assistant," an enthusiastic and capable hippie (better suited to my almost-gone mate Z, who had interviewed her in California. I later found out they exchanged massages on the "interview"). Olivia hangs around in the kitchen in her tight revealing pajamas, prompting me to create a staff manual, including a dress code. She wanders off to Nova Scotia with on-again off-again abusive, controlling, now ex, Z after he blows up.

When I tell Z that I developed feelings for Kent while he was in South America for weeks (with an ex-girlfriend's teenage son, which I did not know at the time), Z loses it, at one point putting his hand around my neck but quickly stopping himself as he realizes what he has done. This brings to mind what criminals in early Island Falls said: They did not want William Sewall's arms around their neck. Strong hands were the only weapon he chose to travel with. I have felt now how a hand around the neck has the potential for being a weapon.

Z's presence makes life dark before he takes off to Nova Scotia with Olivia, later showing up when we have guests, demanding that he use whatever he wants—the phone, the shower. His physical aggression reminds me of a prior incident In New York city when he spit in my face. I find the strength to finally clear him out of my life.

I sit on the shore of the lake, in front of the cabin, sorting out all that has happened, including experiences with lovely guests: a couple from Virginia who usually go to a retreat center in Virgina called Yogaville; a health-food store owner from North Carolina who is going through a divorce; my dear friend Sibyl from England, who had been my roommate in Tokyo in my modeling days, whose father passed away, who is herself getting out of an unhealthy relationship; an enthusiastic New York student who ventured to the Australian outback in search of love, ending up with colitis. And others who passed through our doors that summer.

Having Kent come on board ushers in another era at Sewall House, a partner in wallpapering, serving, and many parts of the puzzle, coming not only with rewards but with challenges, as relationships do.

Chapter 19
KENT ON BOARD

The Guest House

This being human is a guest house.
Every morning a new arrival.
A joy, a depression, a meanness,
some momentary awareness comes
As an unexpected visitor.
Welcome and entertain them all!
Even if they're a crowd of sorrows,
who violently sweep your house
empty of its furniture,
still treat each guest honorably.
He may be clearing you out
for some new delight.
The dark thought, the shame, the malice,
meet them at the door laughing,
and invite them in.
Be grateful for whoever comes,
because each has been sent
as a guide from beyond.

—Rumi

■ **Just Married 2003**

I am the fourth Sewall woman to be married at the Sewall House, the
first my great-grandmother Mary, who was twenty-one and, like me,
went back to work the next day. Kent, his mother, her younger half-
sister (who is my age, forty-eight), and I spend the month before the

marriage cleaning the house, wallpapering the living room. Kent's aunt paints the door from the porch to the kitchen, grumbling about how she thought the old house was going to be in better shape than it is. On the eve of our wedding, Kent's mother wallpapers the second-floor bathroom with paper that has light-blue sketches of claw-foot tubs and old-fashioned sinks.

One of my New York students surprises me with invitations she designed. Kent finds a Parisian wedding dress (with a fragile white cloth butterfly that is sewed on the spaghetti strap the day of the wedding). I had planned on graceful, flowing, less-expensive yoga clothes from an Indian shop in our New York City Little Italy neighborhood, now called Nolita (northern Little Italy). Kent, ever pushing me to spend money beyond my comfort zone, wants this perfect-fit wedding dress (no adjustments needed; it seemed made just for me) from Paris, a still costly sample sale price of $1800, which he discovers in the window of a wedding dress boutique in our Little Italy neighborhood. One friend says his push to make me spend is helping me value myself. Perhaps?

Our June marriage is a family reunion, a tribute to my mother, who is now on oxygen full-time, the cancer that took one breast in her eighties now spread to her lungs. Kent pushes the date because of my mother's health. (She will live until the following April, dying three days short of her 94th birthday) Many things feel pushed, from his moving in when he relocated to NYC, Kent paying no rent while I still had a roommate, to getting married. Kent was thirty-six when he moved in; I was forty-six. Two years later, we are getting married. On the other hand, I feel lucky to have this second chance at a worthwhile union.

The day arrives—June 28, 2003—a sunny, very warm day, with yelping coming from the house behind ours, a small State home for a few mentally slow people. The inhabitant squeals like an owl, which one of our retreat guests later that season will think he is. The ceremony is to take place in the backyard facing the State home. Kent and I wander over in the early morning to ask if something can be done to avoid the possibility of squealing during the ceremony. The squealer comes walking down the hallway, gives Kent a big hug, saying something very loving and innocent, as he is. (which I no longer remember but was touched by). The worker who comes out after him says they have already made plans to take the residents out for ice cream cones at 3 p.m., knowing there would be a wedding—small-town folks' considerate thoughtfulness, to our relief.

At three o'clock, Kent and I stand between two huge old pine trees in the back of the house, the trees giving us shelter, as a marriage is meant to. Fifty guests sit in metal folding chairs borrowed from the Congregational Church (where the stained-glass windows hold the memory of the town founders, my great-great-grandparents Levi and Rebecca Sewall). My sister Nancy, playing on a portable keyboard, flubs the "here comes the bride" song while my eighty-eight-year-old father walks me down the ancient rock laid steps that run off the back of the shed/ now yoga studio. Kent's mother reads in Swedish something she had written while my sister reads the translation (saying I am a glad person and that it was good I get up early!).

The ten-year age difference between me and Kent, with the added factors of Kent's mother having him at a young age and my sister being twelve years my senior, makes his mother and my sister close in age. My nephews both did readings. Kent has a male cousin from Minnesota as his best man. (I have no maid of honor). Many Sewall family members who attend I have rarely seen over the years, cousins, aunts, and uncles who have raised their families, lived their lives, as I ventured searching out into the world. My guests are one student, who videotaped the wedding, another student who photographed it, my ex-roommate Renee, her husband, and my closest friend Denyse (who caught the bouquet amidst tears). They all make the journey from New York City to Northern Maine to attend.

The day after the wedding, a few friends spend the day on the lake with us, another spectacular sunny and warm summer day. Al, a local whose pontoon party boat we travel on, drives the boat, playing old tunes he loves that we dance to in our bathing suits, snacking, swimming, then entertained by a moose our videographer caught on camera—urinating!

The day after our lake tour, our retreat staff arrives. Maureen, the pretty dark-haired woman in her early thirties who had done Public Relations for an art gallery in Upstate New York, had flown to the city to interview with us for the position of house manager. She lasts about ten days. Maureen decides the place is not for her. She departs of her own volition, accusing me of spying on her e-mails, which I had not. Nancy, the massage therapist, whom we interviewed in April when she drove up to meet us from New Hampshire, is going through a divorce. We soon realize that her divorce is causing residual aggression and anger, which becomes directed toward me. She gets angry with me when I ask her to slow down in her yoga practice to protect an injured knee, telling me I am full of fear. She tries to take control of the situation with a technique she learned in therapy: only allowing you to speak when you hold a rock. Kent intervenes, saying that she is being disrespectful to his (new) wife. Kent and I ask her to leave within a few days.

On the other hand, Leda, natural foods chef to Conan O'Brien, is quiet and sweet, referred to us by my photographer friend Carla, who photographed our wedding. We discover that our chef has Chronic Fatigue Syndrome. She cooks well, staying with me through the whole season after Kent goes back to school in the fall in pursuit of his music degree at City College. Sara, Leda's adorable friend, has booked four weeks as Leda's assistant, but stays six weeks. Years later, she tells me it was the most peaceful time of her life. They work on editing cookbooks together. Leda is quiet with dark hair, has a soft way about her. Sara reminds me of a little girl, wearing her shoulder-length brown hair in pigtails; though in her thirties, she looks sixteen with her glasses and shy smile. All women, all different.

I am teaching yoga to the staff on the day after they all arrive. I am (stupidly) standing directly behind Kent when he attempts a headstand, kicks up his legs to the wall, one foot knocking hard into me, blood bursting from my nose. The pain of receiving the impact of his kick releases all the pent-up emotion of getting married and going right into work mode for another season, two emotionally charged unknowns. I burst into tears, blurting out amidst the tears, "I can't do this!"

I wonder what my mind was thinking—the marriage? The uncertainty of each season at the retreat? Or both? What can I "not do?"

In your Amours, you should prefer an OLDER woman [or so it seemed!].

1. They have more knowledge of the world and their mind is better stored with observations.

2. Because when a woman ceases to be handsome, they study to be good.

3. There is no hazard of children.

4. The lower parts continue to be as plimp as ever [OK, it is *plump*, but *plimp* is kind of a fun word for it!].

…They are so grateful!

—Benjamin Franklin, June 25, 1745

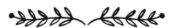

Before Maureen's departure, she came to me on a rainy evening saying there was a man at the front door looking for a B&B. She said he looked a little "different."- plus he was barefoot. He was African-American. Northern Maine is about as homogenous as it gets, with very few minorities at the time except for the migrant workers that were hired by the logging companies to clear brush.

Kent and I went to meet him, realizing he was homeless, albeit clean. Wet from the rain, we offered him a bath. He offered us a (nonexistent) check.

While he was bathing, we decided to offer him the upper garage, where Kent had slept in 2001 during his work-study (before he became the man of the house). The mattress was soft; there was no plumbing. We gave him a slop pot like the one we had in our space (which also had no plumbing, as we slept in the unfinished second floor of the shed that was the renovated yoga studio on its first floor).

When we gathered for dinner, using our best china for Kent's birthday, the girls expressed concern that we had allowed this man to stay even though he was locked out of the house in the upper garage space. To allay the girls' fears, we called the closest police station, twenty-eight miles north in Houlton. The police told us they knew of him, that he had a petty theft record in Georgia but had not hurt anyone.

Kent brought our guest some of his birthday fish soup. He thanked us. We then all went to bed.

In the morning, Kent offered the man more food. The man asked if there was work that he could do for us. Though we told him no, he thanked us again, saying that no one had been this kind to him. He told us he was estranged from his mother and sister but did not tell us why.

He asked if we had a hand mirror so he could groom himself so we brought him one. He sat on the porch, grooming his hair, talking about Jesus in an incoherent fashion, gifting us a small wooden cross. He spent a few more days near the river across from the house, preaching loudly at the town square (more incoherence), then was run off by the town drunk, who yelled some racial slurs at him. The last time I saw him, he was walking I-95 north, barefoot, wearing the red sweatpants I had given him.

When I told my mother this story, asking if she thought we had been unfair to the women we were responsible for in our household, my mother said, "Your great-grandfather would have done the same thing," thus acknowledging that I was carrying on the legacy of the house. Sewall House had been an informal inn for all who passed and needed rest, spilling into the barns and garage when forty men had slept here to build the railroad. For this soul who visited us on Kent's birthday, the tradition continued.

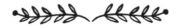

"If you don't see God in all, you don't see God at all."

—Yogi Bhajan

■ Reflections on an Unlikely Friendship
Like the One Between TR and Bill Sewall—
Eddie: Healthy vs. Broken Boundaries

"The true measure of a man is how he treats someone who can do him absolutely no good."

—Ann Landers

It is 1999. I am forty-four years old. In my yoga life this year I begin other form other forms of yoga than Kundalini, including Ashtanga and Dharmayoga. This is also a year my body relented, with the following story of my unusual friendship with Eddie, who was with me in 1999 when I went for treatment for the tumor growing in my bladder, my body I felt relenting to some of the harshness of life. Even failures can turn into winners", I rationalize to myself as I walk into the clinic that day. The things I had put into my body to this point, both physically and psychically, had created harm, a warning. I am treating the wake-up call from the body which has culminated in this moment, reminding me I am still acting out of **naivety**, the lesson being that it is time to finally grow up.

A young man from Long Island ran a tiny bagel shop on Spring Street near my apartment. I met Eddie there. The first time, I was with Z, who made conversation with Eddie (as he would with almost anyone). When Z disappeared on his worldwide travels and adventures (which often included hooking up with other women), I developed a ritual of going to the bagel shop to assuage the loneliness of my empty apartment. I was in my early forties. Eddie would be there, sitting at the counter where Z and I had met him, sad drooping eyes, lack of teeth, the aura of someone for whom life had not been easy. As I got to know Eddie, I discovered his failed marriages, alcoholism, jail, working as a printer, a man now living on social security in a men's hotel in the Bowery, where the other men asked how Eddie and I had become unlikely friends. We developed this recognition of mutual loneliness, which grew into a trusted friendship over shared breakfasts.

In 1998, I asked Eddie to stay with my cat in my apartment while I was in Maine. My next-door neighbor remarked, "You choose odd friends."

I took Eddie for who he was, not what he was. I trusted him.

During the summer of 1999, I invited Eddie to spend a month in Maine, not yet grasping the totality of what I had taken on in buying Sewall House to create an actual retreat business.

Eddie suffered from emphysema, a result of years of smoking unfiltered cigarettes; he'd had sixteen surgeries for various things, including a heart bypass, after which I had visited him in Intensive Care. His body was quite broken; his spirit intact. While in Maine, he would wander to the town coffee shop in the morning, developing acquaintances with locals, including a Vietnam vet named Floyd, who walked with a limp.

Eddie was a perfect candidate for Healing Touch as practiced by my dear friend Pintki from New Mexico. I met Pintki while teaching Kundalini yoga at the Omni health club on summer weekends at the Hamptons, a coastal area wealthy New Yorkers escaped to in the hot summers. I brought Pintki to Maine as a guest healer to inaugurate the yoga studio at Sewall House. Healing Touch is a technique that works with the energy centers along the spine called chakras. A pendulum is held over each chakra (energy area along the spine) to see if it is healthy, then healing energy from the practitioner is given as needed. It was developed by a nurse, which gives its esoteric essence more legitimacy. Pintki's sensitivity identified the offensive smell of anesthesia from so many surgeries in Eddie's system.

When she tested my energy with her pendulum, she said she would not be able to work on my pelvic area, as there was something too intense going on there. She did not know about the recurrent urinary tract infections over the past two years as my relationship with Z became more emotionally difficult. (Once, in my early thirties, I'd had a kidney infection, which I believed stemmed from fearful emotions and confused sexuality. When I paid the receptionist at the doctor's office where I had the infection treated, she looked up and said, "You don't have any money, do you?" She didn't mean I was writing a bad check. She went on to say, "The people with money never want to pay up front.")

Eddie accompanied me when I returned to New York City from Maine for the outpatient surgery to remove the growth in my bladder, which Pintki had sensed in my "second chakra". I intuitively knew this bladder growth developed from the unhealthy feelings (and acts) in my romantic relationship. Eddie had observed me and Z in Maine, said he had seen this type of controlling male, warning me that these kinds of relationships often become dangerous. After Eddie took me home from surgery that day, my boundaries were once again violated when Z showed up at my door. He arrived unannounced, not to nurse me but to take advantage of me. It was this kind of toxic treatment I tolerated (instead of removing myself from it) that had caused my body to react and shout out with this abnormal and uncomfortable growth inside me.

The urinary tract infections, which I had never had before, were mostly relieved by this surgery. Occasionally, the emotional recall would bring the subconscious overwhelmingly uncomfortable feelings back, Kent then helping me get through them. With time it subsided. The book *Emotional Intelligence* actually says that contemptuous relationships can cause bladder problems in women. (I hungrily devoured many self-help books, from *Feel the Fear and Do It Anyway*, *The 7 Habits of Highly Effective People*, and *The Road Less Traveled*, to Wayne Dyer and Norman Vincent Peale, to name a few.) In yoga, the pelvis is the feeling and creative center, not only for your sexual energy, but for your desires and your relationships as well, the first relationship being with your parents.

The wonderful Chinese doctor I had said the growth tested benign. He suspected the tumor would not return. Four years later, on my follow-up, he was right.

My friend Eddie died of liver cancer in 2003 in Florida, where he had returned to be with his sister. He had sent me a card for my wedding; he left me a message the night before he died. When I returned his call the next morning, it was too late. My dear friend Eddie, I miss you and our breakfasts over the *New York Post* at the bagel shop and local diner, both places long since closed due to the gentrification of the neighborhood with trendy eateries and boutiques.

■ A Reflection on Dying found at the Sewall House

My dear son,

I feel that I have been called to die, and that the time is drawing near for me to go. I feel perfectly happy and want you to know that I am willing to give up this life. I know that I will soon be with the dear ones that have gone before, and best of all, I will see my dear savior, whom I have always tried to serve. You know what my life has been, that I have lived as near to him as it was possible for me to. Now that the time has come (for me) and God calls, I feel that my work is done and all is well. I know that this will be a comfort to my children and grandchildren, as well as my friends. I feel just as one of you would if you were away for a long time and [were] going home. I want my children to be prepared when God calls them to die, and it is well to be ready always, as it is uncertain when his call will come. I will not write Vene or Gertie, as you are right handy near them and this letter is for you all. I will now bid you all goodbye, and may God be with you.

Your loving father

Written by Caleb Sherman, Mary (Sherman) Sewall's father, (my other great grandfather) to his son Joseph on November 1, 1902.

Chapter 20
HER PARTING WORDS—
"ALMOST AS MUCH..."

My Mother in her eighties

"Behind all your stories is always your mother's story—because here is where yours begins."

—Mitch Albom

"Guard your tongue, for it is highly dangerous; unguarded words can cause terrible distress. A single bad word can destroy a vast quantity of good. A wound caused by fire will eventually heal; but a wound caused by the tongue leaves a scar that never heals."

—Valluva

After forty-nine years, I hear these words. When I do, they are blended with the other word, *Maine*, the thing we share in common, the gift she gave me. If not given comfort and affection from her, I can find it in the place in the woods that she shared with me. I think my mother would have preferred to take her last breath at the cabin, her most beloved place on earth. The summer of 2003, when I was married on June 28th, my mother traveled 500 miles, on oxygen full-time, to be a part of the wedding in the home she loved as much as I do, perhaps more. Aunt Nancy's home. In tribute to Aunt Nancy and Uncle Maurice, my mother had a beautiful sign made when I bought the house that said "Sewall Cunningham Home"—once again, the two of us stubbornly at odds on my decision to name the place simply Sewall House. Amazing as it was that she made the journey to my wedding, she made it again in August, spending eight days at her cabin, willing herself to get there as my father and Cousin Sam helped her struggle over the sloped rocky shore to get to her destination. Then days of sitting and gazing at the lake she loved, from the cabin she loved, tethered to the long cord that fed her oxygen.

April 2004, visiting my mother in her hospital bed, Stamford, Connecticut, just days before her death, approaching her ninety-fourth birthday, which she will miss by three days. Days away from turning ninety-four, her body is ravaged with cancer that went from the breast to the lungs to the blood; my forever seemingly unfeeling mother—sometimes this can be a blessing, as she says she feels no pain. It is a blooming spring day. Things are coming to life. My mother is dying. My mother is confused, reaching for imaginary stockings to put on as she sits on the edge of the bed in her hospital gown, ever the proper woman, wanting to get dressed. She is in her own world, as I have often thought she was, but this other world is taking her in the direction of death, not coping, not living in her unexpressed internal landscape.

A nurse who knows Maine comes in. My father pleads, "Speak to her about Maine," in an effort to bring her back to this reality and our shared world.

"You love Maine, don't you, Mrs. Miller?" she asks.

My mother looks up in my direction. "I love Maine almost as much as I love Donna." She smiles like a child.

Within days, she is dead, my father going downstairs to get a bite to eat in his first-floor apartment. She has returned from the hospital to the assisted living on the second floor of their retirement community. Within minutes, he gets a call, saying she is gone. "Just like her," my father says. "She always did things her way."

In that way, my mother and I are alike—fiercely, stubbornly independent.

Her unexpected parting words, can they heal the pains of the past? It seems possible—but is it possible to buffer the words uttered to me in my youth - ringing for a lifetime in my head. "No man will ever love you"; "You are going to the devil." Now instead: "I love Maine almost as much as I love Donna." The great love we shared, the gift she gave me. Maine. It seems a most logical and sacred place to give oneself back to the earth, where she and my father and I will lie.

I had a good mother in many ways. We did not always like each other. We may have loved each other. My mother was the strong silent type in contrast to my passionate emotion and nervous talk. I work to curb my verbosity. I still wear my heart on my sleeve, my mother the opposite, fully reserved, contained, locked closed. I have had to learn boundaries lesson after lesson; my being so full of fire, I can see how that would have been a challenge for her calm proper demeanor.

I think my mother might have liked to live her life like Henry David Thoreau, simply in nature, where she seemed most content, amidst the calm and quiet, the sounds of birds, wind in the trees and waves lapping at the shore. Her favorite place really was mine too, the rustic log cabin on Lake Mattawamkeag, the haven where she took us each summer, escaping the pace and sound of the cities that so stimulated and enamored my father. My parents had similar intellectual interests and values- trustworthy and responsible, caring about the entire world. In this way a match: my father, the thoughtful extrovert, and my mother, the thoughtful introvert. Somewhere damaged, as we all are.

Now she is gone. I feel no great remorse, no huge gap in my life. At her funeral, I speak of being the black sheep. I speak my truth. One man I do not know comes up, saying he likes what I said. He tells me he sells windows. The church in Stamford, Connecticut, famous for its stained glassed fish shaped architecture, fills with two hundred people. A few of my close friends from New York City come. Sewall House constantly reminds me of a mother I admired but could not please (except the one time I remember her blurting out that I was wonderful when I bought Sewall House), loved but never understood where her complexities might have come from, what secrets she might have held. I feel we are now perhaps at peace with each other. She lies in the cemetery in Island Falls. I go visit her. She is near the place that brought her the most peace. I feel in my heart she is guiding from afar; I have heard that people can help us more after they leave the planet. I would like to believe she is doing that. I hear her voice, as she would sing at the cabin, "Oh sun, I love thee, great orb of day, shine on my fairest and light their way," to greet the mornings she loved so while there. I hear you, Mom, I hear you.

From you I draw my independence…
and love of Lake Mattawamkeag, Island Falls Maine.

Photo of me below in the summer of 2018—
like mother, like daughter in Maine.

Wearing cap and pants with Sewall House logo and yogi bhajans.
Words on my shirt: "I do not believe in miracles. I rely on them."

Chapter 21
MORE IN 2005

"I don't want to get to the end of my life and find that I just lived the length of it. I want to have lived the width of it as well."
—Diane Ackerman

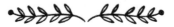

"Aging is not lost youth but a new stage of opportunity and strength."
—Betty Friedan

When I was fifty, one of my longtime Kundalini yoga students who represented photographers got me an interview with *More*, a lifestyle magazine for women aged forty to sixty with a wide circulation and famous women, actresses and the like, gracing the cover. I met the editor, a young woman who exclaimed I was gorgeous! (Reminding me of the scraggly, scrawny tomboy running barefoot around the neighborhood being stopped by the neighbor who made a charcoal drawing of my face, rolled it up, and told me to take it home to my mother. This was the sketch my mother framed and kept for years in her private attic space. It disappeared when they moved out of their home of fifty-four years and reappeared when my sister and I went through the storage unit in my parents' retirement community. I was surprised when I realized my mother had even taken it to their retirement home, having saved only few things she must have cherished.)

For the *More* interview, I do the requisite hair blow and makeup, donning clothes that look the "successful" part, something I aspire to on interviews as a model and actress, not always achieving, sometimes trying too hard.

I had learned some things about presentation since my late thirties, when the head of PR for Saachi and Saachi , a well-known advertising agency in New York City, heard me do an early-morning radio interview on a show called *Rambling with Gambling*. She asked her husband to write my phone number on the mirror with his shaving cream, called me, saying finally she had found a yoga teacher who wasn't crazy. She liked my voice and what I had to say. Crazy, no; still troubled, yes. I taught her Kundalini yoga weekly for a few years. In turn she helped me get into media (prior to social media) by connecting me to editors. This woman got me quoted in national magazines in the early '90s, traveling on national and regional fitness tours using my yoga and nutrition experience to promote Bailey's Light and the health insurance company GHI. She insisted I wear my "war paint," using the knowledge acquired from modeling of how to apply makeup. I was more comfortable "natural," especially since my guru Yogi Bhajan did not believe in makeup. His teachings were directing my life so deeply inward, toward healing and wellness in my early thirties, that makeup, the mask of seduction, felt superficial.

The fitness tour for the health insurance company coincided with the continual urinary tract infections I was suffering at the time, making the interviews challenging as my discomfort could only be described as a feeling of paralyzing anxiety, fear of finally having some real opportunities combined with the insane Z relationship I was trying to maintain much of that time. From 1996 to 2001, I committed to wearing a white turban like those often worn by Kundalini yoga teachers and by Yogi Bhajan. My relationship with this helpful woman, who was, like my acting manager, trying to help me see my worth and beauty, dissolved for no spoken reason. My guess would be a combination of my strange headgear combined with my request that she pay me, insisted upon by Z. A publicist was way beyond my budget. Asking her to pay me was snubbing her generosity of offering her services for barter - with results. Torn between pleasing him and developing the sense that I could make my own decisions, my awkward request for money curtailed her efforts to help further my career, a self-sabotage I had experienced in modeling and acting.

Now, in 2005, at age fifty, the editor of *More* magazine wants to feature me in a one-page section called "Why She Looks So Good." They send a photographer to Maine. The editor interviews me over the phone about my life, extracting pieces for the paragraph that will accompany my photo. The editor asks, among other things, who my favorite designer is, the only designer clothes I have, given to me by my ex Parisian boyfriend Dino's *Elle* magazine editor wife when I was forty. I wear them still ten years later -and still have some as I edit this at age sixty! I tell the editor about leaving my first marriage, about breaking my back skydiving; I leave out the anorexia, talk about my nutrition, the modeling, the acting, and now being a retreat owner. She said the interview would take thirty minutes; she speaks with me for forty-five. A few minutes after we hang up, she calls back.

"I just wondered," she says, "so many women stagnate in a marriage or a career and you have done so many things. What motivated you to do this?"

"Fear," I answer, "I am constantly trying to get rid of my fear."

"TO CONQUER FEAR IS THE BEGINNING OF WISDOM"
—Bertrand Russell

Life, I have discovered, for me is a spiritual quest more than a material quest. I thought as a model, or as an actress, I could make large sums of money, parlaying it into a business to do more good for the world. The spiritual quest, facing my fear, was the thing I grew from, the rich lessons learned, shared with others in the end not about creating great financial resources. In 2005, at age fifty, I have taught thousands of people yoga and meditation, the thing that healed and inspired me. "Why She Looks So Good" reminded me of the features the PR barter student woman had gotten me in various publications in the early 1990s, making a difference in my own small way, as my great-grandfather had done before me.

Chapter 22
2008/2009

■ July 4, 2008: Notes on Guests and Things

We have a full house. Growth for us, a disappointment for two re-peat guests. Anna and Michael want silence at breakfast, saying they feel obligated to socialize with the few other guests; yikes—our guests judge us over whether we have too few or too many people. Dealing with the perceptions and projections of our guests is inter-esting, often helpful, or sometimes critical. They suggest buffet lunch. Yikes. Financial obligations seem to be piling up, but it always feels that way. Each season gets better. Each year gets better—affirm. We are a small retreat: How can Anna and Michael complain about four other people? Isn't part of spiritual growth learning how to deal with others? A.M. class Anna and Michael say is only sixty-five minutes, that we are shortchanging them from the 90 minutes scheduled. Downstairs bathroom—we did promise; we don't have the $—oh dear.

Anna, a young social worker who teaches yoga, Michael her friend, a man who works for Broadway Cares. She does her own thing during class, moving quickly as I have others hold the postures. She is rushing. I asked them before class what they wanted. They said anything. I want to handle the fact that her energy is distracting in our small group with two teacher trainers in the class. I try to be posi-tive, suggesting she might want to teach the next morning in a pace that works for her. She rolls up her mat, walks out. In tears after class, she says I have shamed her. The energy is awful. I try to get it back on track. Anna and Michael go to Baxter State Park all day the next day, leave a day early with the excuse that they have a friend to meet in Bar Harbor. Anna takes herself off our e-newsletter list, then sends a card wishing Sewall House well. During this stay, she is thinner, hardly eating. I notice the odd food behaviors of an eating disorder; she says she is constipated, that is why she had to move faster in class. I too was constipated when I had anorexia, emotionally and physically not processing or letting go. You cannot please all complicated humans, because we are all complicated humans.

■ **Season 2008, others come, too.**

● The Russian Group—Leotid, Baya, Bill, Fahina, Bella

Getting out of the car, Baya, who had studied Kundalini with me in New York City: "What happened to you? You were such an angel." I greet the group in colorful hatha yoga clothes instead of my Kundalini yoga turban and white clothes as I did at the yoga studio Golden Bridge in New York City where Baya studied with me.

● Tatiana and Natalie

Tatiana, a young woman I met me at the Open Center, a well-established alternative learning center in New York City where I was teaching Kundalini. She brings her older aunt with her. They had Russian accents, so much fun "My best vacation ever," she smiles as she leaves but has not returned. "So many beans!" Summer of Russians!

● The couples

PETER AND BARBARA: no-oil Peter.
Peter believes that absolutely zero oil in your diet prevents cancer and heart disease. He is painfully thin, another form of eating disorder? He even makes his own vegetable stock to avoid oil at home, eats little of our food for this reason.

ANN AND ARNIE: sculpture and entertainment producer.
Fun couple who say they should bring some other couples back with them but never do.

ANITA AND RICK: three-year-old; most hidden.
She is the daughter of a real estate mogul in New York City, he a model, and their beautiful aggressive boy, possibly with ADHD?

GREG AND VICTORIA, who knows me from Open Center as well, adorable; he a country musician who works with computers, she teaches hatha yoga. You would never guess she has an ileostomy.

CHARLIE AND JENNY: Cute young couple; she works with children.

● The friends
LINDA AND SUZANNE, who had worked in Rwanda together.
MICHAEL, ANNA AND RITA, returnees reuniting- Rita met Michael and Anna at Sewall House.

● The solos
JESSICA, JOAN, FELICIA, BONNIE, KATHY, NANCY, PEGGY, AND OTHERS—all with their own stories:

Jessica, a young photographer with a good career.

Joan left publishing to work at an orphanage in Cambodia in her mid forties.

Felicia, a social worker who studied with me twenty years ago and has reappeared, practicing Buddhism, doing her chants diligently day and night.

Shira, mother from California going through a divorce.

Sanna, a quiet, sweet young girl from Finland.

Kasandra, a beautiful dark-haired raven from Italy.

And others, each with their own reasons for coming to Sewall House.

Just a quick shot of the many stories that have passed through our doors since we opened in 1997:

■ September 4, 2008: Nature Musings on My Beloved Lake

From one of the brief moments I am able to escape the responsibilities of the retreat to be at the cabin—the contrast between serving others with my energy and time and simply *being*.

It feels like a fairytale;
Flawlessly calm water,
Fish hopping all around me—not sure what it means.

Just watched Mister Eagle fishing but to no avail; now the fish are all around me in the middle of the lake. Deep dark waters. They are jumping around me in numbers.

So calm today that you can hear distant machines, five miles up the lake bulldozing, TOO BAD.

Sitting in the canoe, no movement, except the fish and my pen. Headed out toward Big Island in the canoe at 7:15 a.m. after best night's sleep in months. 6 a.m. woke to dreams of violence, but now don't remember them. Headed out and spotted a moose grazing in the reeds in the East Cove, headed to her in the canoe, observed until she gracefully exited the water, where she was waist deep. She trots off—impressive how graceful those large awkward-looking animals can be.

Loons calling their forlorn call, conversing in small short tones that I cannot decipher. Laughing like a loon. I love the loons.

Last fall, a writer for *Shape* magazine contacted us. Though the fact-check was off, saying we were "on" a lake (we are *near*) and on "several" acres (we are on *one* acre), the magazine has a circulation of two million. This same season (2009), I write an article for *Fityoga* called "A Day in the Life of a Retreat Owner." They add that I had the "courage" to buy my great-grandfather's home, facing fears and hopes, courage that propelled me to run off to Europe or jump out of an airplane. Beyond the fear exists the buried thrill of the unknown; fear is excitement in need of an attitude adjustment.

In 2009, we are chosen one of the top ten retreats worldwide by an online site called Gayot (the same ten retreats in 2010 but not thereafter), which helps our online ranking immensely. Despite being the second summer of an economic recession and airfares to Bangor sky-high, 2009 is our best season to date, Sewall House showing up on the first page of the search engines, often at the top.

With Obama as president, our country in a recession, we apply for our first business loan. We get accepted but decide against the 7.5% interest, the house as collateral, monthly payments that will be beyond our reach. We had hoped to add an extra public use bathroom for the first floor and finish up the large raw space above the yoga studio where we sleep in the summer months. We have ideas to add a deck and hot tub, to upgrade the boiler, plus the chimneys need repair. Our business grows exponentially from 2006 through 2009. Expansion seemed logical, yet the risk of the loan does not.

Kent draws his first "salary" from Sewall House in summer 2008, purchasing a home music studio. Along with the financial responsibility, every January my thoughts turn to finding staff, wondering about guests, the website, our e-newsletters, and more—continuing to learn to "feel the fear and do it anyway," watching the business evolve.

***

"Until one is committed, there is hesitancy, the chance to draw back— Concerning all acts of initiative (and creation), there is one elementary truth that ignorance of which kills countless ideas and splendid plans: that the moment one definitely commits oneself, then Providence moves too. All sorts of things occur to help one that would never otherwise have occurred. A whole stream of events issues from the decision, raising in one's favor all manner of unforeseen incidents and meetings and material assistance, which no man could have dreamed would have come his way. Whatever you can do, or dream you can do, begin it. Boldness has genius, power, and magic in it. Begin it now."

—Some attribute this to John Anster's 1835 translation of *Faust*.

■ **November 16, 2009**
(year Sewall House is featured in Shape magazine)

An amazing season at Sewall House. From a young college couple from Alabama/Tennessee to several adults who do interesting work in DC, to a retired Army woman now working with veterans in Arizona, a wide array of interesting people found their way to us, as well as a few repeats: Cyndi, a mother from Pittsfield, Maine, who first came to us grieving the loss of her own mother, becomes an annual devotee; Kim Gold, a mother who brings her two young adopted Asian daughters; and Anne Marie, who had, like most, found us on the Internet, driving the distance from Massachusetts to visit Sewall House on weekends.

We befriend a local ten-year-old named Sierra, who comes to a free class for children [see her poem in Chapter 9], Kent's mother, Inga, repeats her three-month stay, again looking great when she leaves but feeling more homesick this time. I could see her trying to make the most of it *BUT…*! She accidentally smashes one of my great-grandparents' serving dishes, so sullen the whole day—like she was mad at us! Don't we humans all handle emotions interestingly? Inga helps us toward our next phase of growth, as does smiling work study Deb, the Australian who has studied with me at HB Acting School, where I had large Kundalini yoga classes in the early '90s; Deb rediscovers me at New York Sports Club.

As I approach my fifty-fifth birthday, people continue to weave in and out of my life. No longer enveloped in the tight skin of youth, there is some advantage to the changes life hands you when you have seen and known so many people, places, and experiences. The more diversified the life you have lived, the greater these opportunities, the greater the chance of revisiting this place or person at a different phase or with a different perspective gleaned from an experience of the past.

Kent and I create the space for this successful season, including the first teacher training—a total of three people! I never aspired to offer a training class, but chose to tackle the request that was presented by retreat guest Edith, who lives in Bar Harbor, Maine, and loves Kundalini yoga ("I will not come back unless you offer a training," she writes in our guest book). The world is full of teacher trainings. I had been grandfathered in, first to the Kundalini yoga organization 3HO in the early '90s through a lengthy exam, and then into the organization that oversaw the trainings, Yoga Alliance.

The first Sewall House 200 Hour teacher training brings Edith, who requested it, and Anne Marie, a Sewall House devotee from Massachusetts whose boyfriend found us online. Anne Marie falls in love with Kundalini yoga. The third woman in the training, named Donna, reads an article I write for *Inner Tapestry* (an alternative health publication in New England for which I wrote a bimonthly yoga column for a dozen years). That, after a phone conversation, combined with our both being named Donna, convinces her to join us. Donna arranges to be off work in the medical field, away from her husband and two children in Southern Maine. The first teacher training is a great experience, broken into three nine-day sessions held in October, February, and May, each season offering a different feeling. Photos show us bundled up in October, with the fall foliage framing the lake in the background as we ready the boat to take the ride to a study day at the cabin. There are photos of us *more* bundled up as we stand on the frozen lake in the snow, kicking our legs up like Rockettes. The last session, we sit in the backyard in lawn chairs with the smell of blooming lilacs for aromatherapy, a great first training experience with three diverse and wonderful women, three different seasons. All the women in the first training are mature women, a great group, the beginning of more trainings to come, each a story in itself, inviting challenges to come for more learning, more growth.

"Humanity is like an enormous spider web, so that if you touch it anywhere, you set the whole thing trembling... As we move around this world and as we act with kindness, perhaps, or with indifference, or with hostility, toward the people we meet, we too are setting the great spider web a-tremble. The life that I touch for good or ill will touch another life, and that in turn another, until who knows where the trembling stops or in what far place and time my touch will be felt. Our lives are linked together. No one is an island."

—Frederick Buechner, 1926

"All of life is a journey; which paths we take, what we look back on, and what we look forward to is up to us. We determine our destination, what kind of road we will take to get there, and how happy we are when we get there."

—From *A Little Book of Happiness*

■ November 2008: Sewall House upon Departure after a Thanksgiving Retreat with One Guest

Today we have breakfast at 8 a.m. after our 6 a.m. yoga Sadhana. Our only guest, Jaquie, a young woman who found us online, is doing the Kundalini training in New York City. She looks out the window and says, "It seems so strange to see someone smoking a cigarette at 8 a.m." (one of the nurse's aides at the house behind us). I agree, adding that it seems odd to see anyone smoking any time.

The contrast between what goes on inside Sewall House walls—breathing exercises, healthy food, Yogi tea, yoga, conscious conversation and communication—and what goes on just across our yard at the State-run residential home. What fate has given the inhabitants their lesser intelligence to function in society yet us a freedom to choose our thoughts, words, and actions every day so different than theirs? What a gift we have to self-evaluate, self-assess, improve ourselves, help others grow. At 9 a.m., I leave Sewall House on the twelve-hour bus ride back to NYC after our tiny Thanksgiving retreat.

It is our first Thanksgiving without Westy, our eighteen-year-old mascot cat, who left us just before this retreat, leaving a hole in the heart as pets do when they depart. Kent diligently took Westy in to the vet for his parting moment, me crying my way up to Maine from New York City on the bus, knowing the time that he is scheduled to be put down, reading a book on the bus ride up to Maine that my father gave me about Dewey, a cat found in a library chute that becomes their mascot. At the moment I imagine Westy is being put down, I hide my tears behind the pages of this book, the sweet story of Dewey the cat further opening my grieving heart.

Today I am on the bus back to New York City watching people get off to have their smokes. I imagine the wasted-looking woman sitting in front of me might be my age. Her eyes are drooping, her hair is long and scraggly. At each stop, she and her partner get off the bus to smoke. Her eyes flirt with the bus driver. When I first get on, I watch her keenly, not knowing that she is traveling with a guy. She gets back on the bus, sits in front of me, then her companion a pot-bellied smoker, joins her. Sitting behind them, I notice that the tips of his ears are dark, like the circles under his eyes. I have heard that the outer ear represents the internal organs. Are they a reflection of what is going on inside his body? I feel an urge to tell him to stop smoking; it is killing him. She rests her head on his shoulder, he wraps his arm around her, talks to someone on his cell phone. I hear something about $9700 and do they need to borrow money. The economy is tanking. Obama just got elected.

Kent had made his phenomenal food for the retreat. I have a peanut butter sandwich along with his parmesan Kalamata olive biscuits, all of it home made, including the popular peanut butter he sells to guests.

Kent has chosen to live in Maine this winter. I feel grateful for what NYC offers me as a teacher and student yet I miss the embrace of the Sewall House energy. I imagine spending a winter there. I love teaching yoga, earning a living from it in NYC; it pays bills. I miss my husband.

Kent and I plan to create a teacher training in Maine in the winter (mentioned previously), Kent plans a cookbook (created in summer 2010, finished just in time for Christmas), and a mantra CD (never finished). Kent hibernates with our sweet shy black Maine coon cat Shanti and fluffy born blind Lucy, our wonderful cats. We are separated, but connected in our mutual goal of artistic growth and serving at Sewall House.

I am doing my best to practice *Santosha*, the yoga word for contentment.

■ 2008: More Musings on Music, Writing, and Yoga

Sound when stretched is music
Movement when stretched is dance
Mind when stretched is meditation
Life when stretched is celebration
　　　　　　—Shri Shrit Ravshankar

I play music in my yoga classes. In Kundalini yoga classes, the music is recorded by Kundalini yoga artists. Yogi Bhajan told us "a people must have their songs." (so true especially in times of loss or less that require courage). When I teach other forms of yoga like hatha or vinyasa yoga, I play non-Kundalini new-age or spiritual music with Indian chants, often Indian chants in Sanskrit, the ancient language of yoga.

I occasionally make small movements with the music, which come naturally. Whether I am tapping my toes or sitting straight and cross-legged to chant a Kundalini mantra meditation, my impulse to move with the music; it is so inherent that I do not always realize I am doing it. I don't know if this is right or wrong, but I realize it comes from what I feel. As a child, I begged my mother to let me learn to ride horses and play the violin; the violin won. Memories of my amazing violin teacher Dietz Weisman, who I imagine escaped Nazi Germany. Born with perfect pitch (the ability to identify what a note is by just hearing it played on a piano for example- even 2 notes together) he retrained me from tone deafness with his caring teaching, while envying my ability to whistle through my teeth, as he whistled through puckered lips all day while teaching, tiring his face muscles by end of day. I played violin for eight years, ages nine to seventeen, including in a junior philharmonic, as well as three years of singing and piano lessons from the person who also directed the choir at the Presbyterian Church my parents attended, the director insisting we children be a part of the choir. Today, yoga is my music. Others attend concerts or listen to their gadgets on the subway. Music stimulates the whole brain. In the elderly whose minds are going, often all they remember are songs.

In conversation with a student after a yoga class at the New York Sports Club, he mentions that he just finished writing "another" book. I tell him that I write articles, am trying to finish a book. "Write like you teach," he says. "Did you notice how you move and dance as you teach? Put that into your writing." Another student tells me I seem joyful as I move to the music while I teach. Shouldn't we all move joyfully to the music within? Maybe that is why Yogi Bhajan had us dance so much: "Sweat and laugh every day," he said. Dancing is good for the glands. Dancing is like an inner smile. An outer smile stimulates hormones that maintain health. The glands produce the hormones that keep us healthy. Yogi Bhajan called the glands the guardians to our health. Glands tell you when your body's balance is on or off. Milk appeared from my nipples when I was stressed out by the pressure from Z for me to get pregnant at forty, something I had never wanted to do with any man. The stress stimulated the hormone prolactin, caused by an imbalance of the pituitary, the master gland of the body. Z thought it was a sign that my body wanted to be pregnant. How interesting, the ways that our body speaks to us. How important that we listen and move to and for it, not against it.

As we relaxed after our yoga set at Sewall House this morning, Thanksgiving 2008 retreat, the lines from the song playing struck me: "She is the silent hero of the human race / She has made the entire universe into a better place."

It brought tears to my eyes as I thought about Aunt Nancy, the silent hero of Sewall House, loving it, preserving it—like taking care of a beloved child since she could not birth a human child, sharing remembrances of the happy childhood she had in this house when any of us would eagerly listen. I realized that I, like Aunt Nancy, was a Sewall woman who did not birth a child, whose destiny it would be to put all my energies into this house like a parent to a child, to see what music I could create in the rhythm of this challenge, to move with it, to see if I could, as my student George had suggested, bring my rhythm into the telling of the story. George gifted me a writing pen that used ink cartridges, similar to the pens that my ancestors must have dunked into ink to write their wills and other important documents. I find an old-fashioned pen in the safe of the house, the beautiful penmanship of the past, like that on my great great grandfather Levi's will found in the safe, the art of that penmanship lost to modern times.

Chapter 23

SECRETS

Secrets. We all have them. This week our new website launched, eleven years after the first one in 1999. Our original website, though drawing guests, had become cluttered and outdated as we managed to stay on top of the search engines, including Google.

The day the new website goes live, my husband goes on another bender. This time not for one night, as he had on my fiftieth birthday, waking in remorse, jumping back into life sober after an AA meeting. This time it lasts three days—not answering phone calls, occasional strange e-mails. Kent told me when we first got together that he had been in rehab for drugs, been hooked on amphetamines in his twenties, was an alcoholic who no longer "needed" AA. Having no experience with alcoholism I took his words as truth. At my birthday party, two years after we were married, he insisted on having alcohol because "people like to drink." He overruled me on that as he had on purchases and other financial matters. He drank himself into a stupor that night, his personality changing completely. The few close friends still at the party went to a restaurant with me, luckily the only people to notice his switched persona after the party had thinned out. As my few friends and I left him behind, passed out on the bed, to escape to a local restaurant, I feared for my marital future. He woke up remorseful, went to AA that day. He stayed sober for years, until 2009.

Beginning in 2009, during the three winters that Kent lives isolated at Sewall House, relapses begin to occur. Isolation is the worst thing for an alcoholic, something I did not realize.

Kent had become the chef at Sewall House in 2006, his food so well received that he created a cookbook in 2010 on the urging of guests and me. The hundred copies of his cookbook we made sold quickly. Another fifty were promptly printed up by the printing shop in Bangor, the city eighty-eight miles south of us where we also picked people up from the airport. Ostensibly in Maine to produce music—with equipment he spent our earnings on as I no longer saved and we take no salary—the music has not yet transpired. Other "house" projects distract him, he says. Is it wrong? I don't know. He is a seemingly indispensable part of the operations of Sewall House. For three days, though, he has been out of touch, literally and figuratively, while I keep up appearances in New York City teaching yoga, doing my best to inspire and to be inspired to help people manage their lives and their own challenges through my work.

I am fifty-six years old, thinking things are settled after all the years of tumult, of drama. I wake this morning to my Yogi Bhajan calendar on July 7, though today is March 12. Yogi Bhajan's words stare up at me: *If at one frequency you are freaking out, change your energy.* I tell myself, "You will not freak out. You cannot get out of the body but you can change its energy."

I reach out to my closest friends. I reach out to Kent's mother and my sister. I attend my first Al-Anon meeting, a small room in a building on Union Square. There is something comforting in the smallness of the room, like the intimacy of Sewall House with our small groups. I feel completely vulnerable. All day I feel tears in the back of eyes as I walk the streets of New York, doing what I know and love most, teaching yoga, my students having no idea what is welling inside me. I realize the people in this room struggle with the same issues. Our secrets are universal. They must be told.

He comes off the three day bender to return to massage school. I surrender to my practice, to my thoughts, to wait and see if what he says is coming from truth or from alcoholism and manipulation. I feel helpless. Fear thoughts arise, anxiety over the idea that the retreat can fail, I can lose Sewall House. Yoga philosophy tells us to be the same whether we gain or lose—content, nonattached, remembering the divine. Am I there?

When Kent relapses right before our Christmas Retreat, I pay for a therapy session when he comes down to fetch me in New York City. The therapist treats his relapse lightly, a "slip," but drinking a bottle of vodka in one night is more than a *slip* to me. Am I controlling, not empathetic? He wants to go back to this therapist. I tell him I will not pay. I have paid for many things in the ten years we have been together, am no longer able to save, feel as if I have been living on the edge financially—something I am used to—but the edge feels sharper now, when he purchases music equipment while I watch with no say, feeling powerless to affect his choices. Friends say he is hiding in Northern Maine. He is a good man, a capable, gifted man. I feel he is trying to figure out what he wants to be when he grows up at almost forty-seven. I, of all people, should understand this late blooming—but at what cost? Financial? Emotional? He feels resented, under-appreciated. I shut off sexually, partly because I resent being the sole provider in the winter, though he does not see it that way for all the work he does at Sewall House. He says I am a workaholic. I believe if he had his own work, his music or cooking, he would have his own identity, separate and still a part of Sewall House, as my yoga teaching is.

I do as I always do, keep up, looking for solutions to the problems, at least the ones I may be able to solve. I start looking for a cook because Kent decides he no longer wants to cook, telling me three days before I head to Maine for my second small teacher training. They are wonderful women who chose to do this training with me of all the options out there. I know little of the 12 Steps, but I know to take one day at a time.

I attempt to look honestly at myself. Have I substituted spiritual superiority for actual intimacy in a relationship? Stopped my own patterns of promiscuity but remain unresolved in my own ability to truly connect to another person and their needs? It is so simple, so easy to rationalize it into their behavior versus mine, some holier-than-thou attitude that does not repair me or the relationship. I remember the therapist I was seeing in my early thirties saying that relationships were the hardest thing. I look her up. I discover she has died. I wish she were alive.

Chapter 24
SOLD SHORT

I Was Dying
First I was dying to finish high school and start college
And then I was dying to finish college and start working
And then I was dying to marry and have children
And then I was dying for my children to grow older so I could return
   to work
And then I was dying to retire
And now, I am dying, suddenly I realized I forgot how to live.

—Anonymous
(submitted by Nicole Zablocki)

■ **November 20, 2009**

Sewall House had its busiest season yet. We travel to Tuscany Italy in
the fall a second time for a yoga and walking trip, a very different
group than the first time. The first time, we had ten people spanning
the years at Sewall House; this year six. Only three came off our website; we did not know them before the trip unlike our first group. We
stop to visit my friend Sibyl, now a massage therapist in London,
whom I had met when I was in Tokyo, the place I worked the most
as a model but never saw a dime for the effort. Time and time again,
I was sold short and allowed myself to be. Now I have bought Sewall
House, determined not to give up, to see if it is possible to stop the
pattern of being sold short. Through perseverance, Sewall House has
become profitable after ten years. Am I still selling myself short by

not being able to take a salary while yoga grows into a billion-dollar business? (Who would have ever guessed how yoga would grow when I started practicing and then was urged to teach?)

I am back for my winter in New York, reminded that the mental and physical health I have is the most important thing, reminded that being truly sold short is not the worst thing that can happen.

Paula, like Sibyl, is another close friend from my modeling days. Paula, Sibyl, and Donna are the three friends I have kept closest since Paris. All three have visited Sewall House. Paula came in 2006 with her three- and five-year-old daughters. I was Paula's maid of honor at her wedding to a wealthy born-again Christian conservative businessman. Her husband, like many born-again Christians, believes yoga conflicts with their religion. Paula decides to visit Sewall House for ten days while her two boys are at a sleep-away camp in Maine. Her husband makes, as she puts it, ridiculous amounts of money working as a top executive for one of the two largest paper companies in the world. When she visits Sewall House, she has overcome ulcerative colitis by adhering to a gluten-free diet, as well as surgery for a tumor in her ear canal near her brain, a rare form of cancer that has since spread to her spine and lungs. She tells her four children that "Mommy had a small rock removed from her head."

Paula and her girls have ten fun-filled yoga days, the feisty, funny, strong blonde three-year-old and the reserved, gentle, sweet brown-haired five-year-old. We take them on nature outings to the cabin and waterfalls. At first, they fear the outdoors; with exposure, they are excited by it. Paula says they still remember it. When she prepares to leave without paying us a dime for her ten days, it is awkward. I feel hurt because money is always tight while they have so much of it. I have to ask her to at least pay for her massage as she is leaving.

Fast forward to this fall day three years later in NYC. I get an e-mail from Paula asking me if we can meet for breakfast the next day. We arrange to meet at my apartment between teaching commitments, 10:45.

As I approach my apartment building, Paula is waiting, six feet tall, thin, as usual, with a wool cap, sweatpants, and sunglasses, looking like the Paula I know—until she pulls off her wool cap to reveal a tuft of hair. As we enter the building, she asks me how many flights up. Only two, I say. She says, you go ahead, I am kind of slow. She mentions how she gets winded by stairs. Paula is ten years younger than me, like Sibyl. Her translucent beautiful skin, which won her jobs for beauty shots as a model, is looking sadly worn, though she does not look old or as sick as she probably is.

She settles in to have tea as she unfolds her story about being in New York City. She had a whim to contact a friend from thirty years ago who happens to be working at Sloan Kettering. It is not easy to get into this hospital, which specializes in cancer, but she was able to get a consult about an experimental treatment. It would require her being away from her family. She had set in her mind when they said lungs and spine that it meant one tumor in each place. She finds out her lungs alone have eight. She refuses to be away from her children. She says her twelve-year-old son understands best. Her ten-year-old son says angrily, "When is this stupid cancer thing going to be over?" Paula, not the most open book, has opened up to me. She says she has terrible thoughts when she is alone after driving them to school. Paula leaves.

In the spring, she has a vertebra removed. She writes me, saying she remembers that I broke my back and comments on how well I have done. Paula is a trooper. She loves her children. It is all she ever wanted. I am sure if there is any blessing in this, it is that she has the best health care possible.

■ June 11, 2011

Last night I received an e-mail from Paula's husband. Though he and I are polar opposites in our beliefs about things—politics, religion—we have one thing in common: our love for Paula. I had just been sorting through old photos the night before, seeing me and Paula, much younger, much freer, looking very happy amongst friends in my Paris apartment twenty-five years ago. The next evening this e-mail arrived:

Donna,

Wanted to give you a heads-up re: Paula's deteriorating condition. She's been in the hospital since Sat. a.m. The kids made it back from camp to see her. She's not in a lot of pain but still having a tough time breathing.

Peter

And soon after, this one:

Dear Donna,

Dino sent me your mail about Paula. I'm very sad. Could you tell Paula if it is possible, that I'm sure she's gonna be better soon, and as I may come to NY in July I'm going to bring a big brownie with whipped cream from Jo Allen rue Pierre Lescot in Paris just for her. I remember when we had lunch, she didn't want to order one because she wanted to stay slim! But every time I ordered one, I had to share with her!!!! :-))))) I will pray for her and her family. Give her my love kisses.

Alex [one of our dear friends when we all lived in Paris]

Paula died on the full moon, Wednesday, June 15, 2011, leaving her four beloved children and her husband and all of us who loved her in Paris and beyond.

Paula's short life puts life in perspective. Our attitude is everything. I haven't been sold short. Others, it seems, are sold much shorter. Paula, I feel, was truly sold short.

Two years later, Paula's husband remarries, sending me Christmas card updates so I can watch the children grow—and see Paula in them. His mother, who lives in wealthy Greenwich, ends up in the same retirement home as my father in Stamford, Connecticut. I introduce myself but realize she does not recognize anyone, just has the same fake smile pasted on as when she told her grandchildren, "You are not going to yoga camp, you are going to visit Paula's friend Donna." Yoga was a word not to be spoken, (it is against their religious beliefs, so they think) going to Donna's house meant a visit to a friend not a business the friend was running—the least of it all that money not received now that my friend is gone. Little does money matter; the memory of a friendship means much more.

Chapter 25

INSURMOUNTABLE SOUNDS

Written March 19, 2011, on the train back from Connecticut after seeing my dad and moving his things to a smaller storage unit.

When I bought Sewall House in 1997, my mother spent two months on a canvas Army cot, the same type of cot we slept on at the cabin every summer, in a small bedroom on the third floor of the house. My mother delighted in going through Aunt Nancy's accumulated clutter. Since Aunt Nancy never threw anything away, it took multiple sortings and trips to the dump to pick through the canning jars, the barrels full of Easter basket grass, and, among other things, unused sets of glassware. The bedroom closets and drawers were bursting with clothing, some high-quality useable vintage, most outdated and worn out. Weaving through the house contents felt a never ending project, years of excavation. The house and its contents resonated with the accumulated energy of life lived in it over the past 150 years.

So focused on the house, I tuned out the external until 1998. One of my students, Joel, who had owned a small B&B in Florida, came to visit. Joel did a meticulous inventory of the entire house, creating a guide for needed improvements, suggestions for additional bathrooms, upgrading electricity, and more. Joel also noticed there was a constant drone that did not stop nor lessen in the dead of night.

The town was supported by a small old starch factory owned by an international corporation called National Starch. Ten percent of the town was employed there. Those who lived within range of the drone were accustomed to the white noise that put food on their tables in an area with few employment possibilities.

The plant had once been a potato factory, twenty-five years before, a logical thing for Aroostook County, which is known for its potato farms. At the turn of the twentieth century, the location had been a tannery. The last one of the existing row of houses for the tannery employees, painted a nondescript gray, stood opposite Sewall House. It was beside the old Grange, now a place, Sam told us, where wandering cats were known to enter, fall into deep places, never to return.

Until Joel questioned me, I had not noticed the sound, strange since I am a noise-sensitive person, often sleeping with earplugs (which had led to exploratory surgery in 1995, almost killing my cat Westy, who played with the ear plugs, which resulted in consuming two of the spongy things). Joel asks for a tour of the starch factory, returning excited. Joel is assured that for $2000 a sound-barrier wall like the ones near airports and highways can be built to deflect the noise. Rumors fly that I had sent a spy, which soon expands to the rumor that I am trying to close the factory.

I write a letter to the corporate headquarters in Indiana explaining that I have purchased the family home in hopes of preserving its history, part of the town history, creating a retreat to host the general public. They respond, setting up a meeting with the manager of the local plant.

My friend Sibyl is visiting from England at the time of the starch factory meeting. (She is the friend, Tokyo modeling room mate, with whom I had written a list of all the men I had slept with, like a shopping list.) The day of my meeting, Z is on hand but does not accompany me. I had wanted to buy the house with him. Later I would be grateful we had kept separate legal lives.

I put on an ankle-length flowered dress that my friend Donna had given me. I walk over to the factory, a stone's throw away. A tall gray-haired reserved local man named Peter greets me pleasantly. A few minutes later, the manager enters, dressed in a polyester button-down shirt that is *un*buttoned enough to see the gold chain swimming in his chest hair. I feel like I am in a New Jersey disco. I find out later that he is from Jersey. The vulture does not hesitate in his attack.

Immediately, he lights into me. "How dare you contact the main headquarters. Who do you think you are? You are not even a local. [True, but my family did found the town.] How dare you question the noise? You are not a full-time resident, and the town has no problem with the noise, which, besides it all, is within EPA standards," he rants at me. [Later, the State told me it wasn't, but the town had the jurisdiction.] "Besides," he adds, "I have the report in hand to prove it."

I ask if I can have a copy of the report. He barks "No!". Meeting over. The taxes from the factory support the town, as do the jobs. Shaken, I had expected the meeting to be an amicable discussion of the possibility of installing an inexpensive noise wall.

The loud white noise bothers some guests; others, it doesn't. The ones tuned into it, like I am now, are having problems sleeping, being in the yard or on the porch. One guest thinks it is a stuck car alarm, while another thinks we pipe the yoga sound *om* into the house! I begin to obsess over it, let it drive me crazy, worrying—beyond my fears about finances—about the fate of the retreat.

I speak to a sound specialist in Maine, who knows the factory because he fishes at Mattawamkeag Lake. He tells me their equipment is ancient. Unfortunately, the company has no intention of making upgrades because he informs me that would solve the problem. I put earplugs in each room, avoid mentioning it in conversation, wondering if guests are driven crazy by it. I feel helpless, a familiar anxious uncomfortable feeling I have had in relationships, careers, and with money.

In August 2007, I am at the local grocery store. I see Nancy, the owner of a local restaurant. Nancy moved from Rhode Island to create an acclaimed restaurant in town with her Newport , Rhode Island chef boyfriend around the same time I bought Sewall House. Nancy asks me how things are going. I tell her I am concerned because we have not had bookings for a few weeks, adding that the starch factory noise is not helping. Nancy says, "They have a new manager named Alan who is really cool. You might contact them again. The other guy is gone."

There has been talk of the factory closing, already some cutbacks, people laid off. The noise, however, is going strong 24/7. Since my last meeting at the factory, Sewall House has been featured in national magazines like Instyle, Shape and Travel & Leisure. This time around I am married to a man who would help me face a bully. Kent and I approach the new manager, first with a well-thought-out letter, which results in a meeting. Alan Martin is no bully, as Nancy said. He says he will work with us on it. We walk around the perimeter, noting where the loudest noises are. He is able to do some small things to bring the noise level down so that the season is quieter, though the noise is still 24/7.

In 2010, sad for the town but not for the retreat, the factory closes. The town sells it for a dollar. The location is now a scrap metal business, not pretty to view but silent at least.

Another disturbance arises, the bane of my existence for 2008 and 2009. After much stress and many sleepless nights, patient perseverance again prevails, winning the reward of silence.

The town is alcohol-free when I purchase Sewall House in 1997. In 2002, for the first time since the town was formed in 1845, the Nina Sawyer building, diagonally across the street from Sewall House, a large green building that was the library when I was a child, becomes a bar. (Nina Sawyer was Aunt Nancy's best friend who had written a history of Island Falls.) My great-grandfather, a devout Christian and a prohibitionist, was undoubtedly turning over in his grave.

The town needs all the commerce it can squeeze out of the tiny population. The location of the old library, a place of quiet, becomes the Forever Young Saloon. For the first few years, with various managers, the bar is contained. Our chef/massage therapist enjoys moose meatballs in the fall of 2002 at the Forever Young Saloon, a novel Northern Maine cuisine made from a local woman's first moose kill. Vegetarian since my early twenties, I have by this time also given up social drinking, a result of Kent being in my life with his admission that he is an alcoholic. Ever since I started doing Kundalini yoga in 1985, recreational drugs and social drinking have not been a part of the spiritual path that Yogi Bhajan teaches (Though he says spirituality cannot be taught but rather is "caught" like catching a cold!). I gradually have given up alcohol and recreational marijuana, feeling more clear and alive as a result. No booze or meatballs at the saloon for me.

In 2008, the new manager of the saloon adds live bands one weekend a month. In a town that is in the middle of nowhere, dead quiet by 9 p.m., having a band start up at 10 p.m. across the street, especially with a booming bass, is far from ideal. The drunks fight on the street, staying out until after the bar closes, a guaranteed time of screeching tires with drunken shouting. One work-study guest who is with us for two weeks thinks a woman is being raped when she hears screaming at 3:30 a.m. She attends the town meeting to testify. The bar manager says he will do the best he can to contain the situation. It does not change. The bands are only there once a month, but the bar is open every weekend. I hold my breath every weekend. On any given weekend, the music and fighting get out of hand.

Things go from bad to worse when the manager of the bar is fired. The following summer, 2009, the owner puts his twenty-four-year-old son, who has a record for drug possession, in charge of the place. Rumors fly that drugs are being sold. The town officers, whom we ask for help as we did the prior summer, are approached by me and the couple who lives next door to the bar. Besides the noise levels, the couple is upset that their flower beds were urinated on while salacious activities were taking place in their driveway. The bands have become more frequent while the decibel level rise beyond legal limits, forcing the couple, who live next to the bar, to leave their house on weekends. Many a weekend night, I am calling the State Police. We have no local sheriff. When my great-grandfather was the sheriff, the local criminals said they wanted to avoid having Bill Sewall's huge hands around their neck. His namesake, my mother's cousin Bill, had also been sheriff and had hands the size of a ham (he could get a quarter through his wedding ring and was said to be the strongest man in the county). The couple living next to the bar gets a lawyer.

The couple who lived next to the bar (and across from us) and I become allies, calling the State Police when the noise levels are up or brawling and screaming occurs. We attend town meetings, where I am bullied by the bar owners, who say I am the reason the starch factory that supported the town has closed, which of course is not true.

In July of 2010, the bar reopens, having closed down the previous September, which I hoped was for good. The bar opens with a bang with a band on July 4th weekend. This time they are open every night. The word around town is that money is going out faster than it is coming in. Within a month, they are closed again. A for sale sign goes up. Patience, perseverance, and dedication prevail. The bar is done.

2009 was our best year at the retreat to date, ten years after the website was launched. We were glad to report to our repeat guests that the factory and bar had closed. Many in 2010 were new guests, drawn from our high ranking on Google, diverse guests from a wide range of geographic locations and walks of life.

As 2011 approaches, more reviews are added on Trip Advisor from satisfied guests. We joined Trip Advisor in 2009, the year a young schoolteacher from DC (who teaches at the school President Obama's girls attend), told us about the site. She writes our first positive review. These reviews build, helping people who find the Sewall House site choose us as the world of yoga retreats expands, our internet ranking slipping, except in more specialized searches like "Maine yoga retreats" or "new England as opposed to the general search for yoga retreat that we were so highly ranked from 2009-2011. Thousands of yoga retreats saturate the market.

In 1999, a fellow New York Sports Club yoga teacher, Vince, called when he saw me on *Good Morning America*—in Penn Station at 5 a.m. with the weather guys, demonstrating and talking about plow, a yoga pose where you lie down and throw your legs over your head. Demonstrating on the cold hard floor of the train station, I was representing a health club franchise I taught yoga for, New York Sports Club. Vince asked if I would like to create a website, which I knew nothing about, but I thought it might help the Sewall House. What I did not realize is that this website would be the ticket to Sewall House's survival and success. In 2010, a woman contacted us from a company that did websites for B&B's. She had seen our listing in a small feature in the *Boston Globe* online. Instead of hiring her to revamp our website, though we loved her work, we were able to barter with Bradley, a student who attended my Kundalini yoga class at NYSC. He had mentioned that he worked for the web department at his job.

I convinced Kent, who was now spending winters in Maine, that I thought Bradley would be great to upgrade the website. Kent mistook this as my not respecting or including him. I trusted people until proven otherwise, while Kent needed people to prove their worth before he would trust them. The differences between us seemed to create a balance, me learning lessons that boundaries were sometimes better than blind trust, which was different from intuition. Blind trust, not always a good thing, had carried me through so much of my wandering in Europe yet sabotaged me with situations like the careless Sewall House caretaker.

I prevailed about having Bradley do the site. Like many steps that developed in the gradual evolution of the Sewall House, Bradley worked patiently with me and Kent. The new website was easier to navigate, including digital photos we had been taking since 2003—photos of the natural surroundings and shots of guests enjoying various activities from eating to swimming and kayaking, from doing yoga to hiking.

Other aspects of running a viable business were always on our minds, as we evaluated ideas that would better serve our guests. For example, a bathroom on the ground floor near the kitchen and the yoga studio would have been an improvement and a huge convenience for both us and our guests, but the estimate was $20,000. It would have to wait. And every spring, gripping anxiety crept in as I speculated on a new season and all the aspects of what we were doing. Would we find staff? Would guests find us? Each season, each situation was a lesson, often questioning myself and my ability to keep things going. Giving up was not an option. I was committed to the service and healing of others at Sewall House, as it had done for others long before me, because I believed in how yoga and meditation had helped pull me into a healthier direction in my own life. If I had seen the larger picture and challenges that running Sewall House entailed, my fear might have stopped me from taking it on. When I was fifty-six, my fifteenth year of commitment to Sewall House, my father understood the feelings I was dealing with, even as I loved running the retreat, (dichotomy once again!) saying I had "tenacity in the face of adversity".

Spring 2011 rolled around. We were having our second teacher training. With the house full, we started to think again about the need for a downstairs public bathroom. People often asked where the bathroom was on the first floor, and, with apologies, we sent them to the second floor.

We had added a metal roof two summers before (deciding against redoing a shingled roof as we had done on the wraparound porch) and repaired one of the three chimneys in 2010. As with any home, there was always "something". The uncertain finances continued to feel daunting, along with the staff issues, the house itself, serving the guests and their needs. We were no longer given permission to sublet our rent stabilized New York apartment, which had been a helpful buffer from 2003 to 2006 and again in 2008–2009. We were keeping up, the mantra of Yogi Bhajan's Kundalini yoga- "Keep up and you will be kept up." The challenge was to keep moving forward. Kent was a good partner in the endeavor, despite the alcoholic relapses, the challenges of our relationship, and my fears around money. That spring I was working on my mind with yoga and morning meditation, reading the yoga sutras interpretation by Swami Satchidananada. (The yoga sutras are the basis of yoga, written by the sage, Patanjali, primarily a treatise on "threads" of the mind written in 400 BC. A New York City student gifted me the book, the e-mail that follows this section forthcoming with the gift.)

In 2011, when I mentioned in passing that we were going to have the house filled with a group of schoolteachers, which meant guests overflowing into the uper-rustic barn, my dear old dad came forth with an advance on what I would inherit. We wanted a first-floor bathroom that looked like part of the house instead of part of the garage it would be located in.

We envisioned this bathroom for years, Kent buying me a book on bathrooms with photos for us to envision from. With an acrylic claw-foot tub, the new bathroom would be the most spacious of all four bathrooms, perfect for the high traffic of kitchen staff, massage therapists, and guests it was nearby. After years of sneaking to the third floor in the early morning while guests slept, Kent and I finally had a bathroom more convenient to our sleeping space above the yoga studio. Kent was able to stretch the $20,000 budget to create a pantry room in a space opposite the new bathroom for the two refrigerators that had been on the garage landing, the project completed just in time for the group of teachers, including two who stayed in the barn and could access the new bathroom via a back door.

What follows is the counsel from my student who gave me the yoga sutras:

> It felt sooooooo good to see you today… and to practice under your care! In a way, I'm sort of glad I missed last week because my going today really underscored the reason why —at least for me—the practice is so crucial. Thank you, too, so much (!) for hounding me and forcefully insisting that I do the Sat Kriya in the morning (chanting practice that pumps the belly for inner strength, particularly nerve strength). The reason I haven't been able to do that is because I've been trying to still do my

meditation (as it is, I've had to cut down on the time for that in half already). As a "baby step" strategy, I'll try to play around with either doing meditation one day and Sat Kriya the next, or I'll see if I can cut down on the meditation a bit more and do both each day. Anyway, I'll keep trying different permutations. Thank you, again, for insisting.

You asked me earlier what one has to do to manifest BIG. I guess your question stuck with me because I noticed something at the end of class. When you were talking about the retreat house in Maine, you introduced it as "we have a small retreat house up in Maine" (or words to that effect). You might want to rethink using the word "small." Looking back, this is how you've always introduced it—I just made the connection to your question today, though. You don't have to say it's "big," but how about "an amazing" or "a successful" or "a magnificent" or "a life-changing" or "a really, really great" or "an awesome" or "a mind-blowing" or "a thriving" or "a flourishing" or "a prosperous" or "an out-of-this-world" you get the point … "retreat house."

At first I thought to myself that the word change [would be] for other people to hear and believe. But … as I'm sure you've realized by now … and to tie it into your description of your workshop when you said it was about the congruence of external and internal … it may be an indication of what you think/feel about the retreat house business … which is what the Universe is giving you.

You may also want to consider doing the above for when you describe your private lessons. I think you mentioned when we were on the couch that you had a "few" private students. What about "a growing number of" or "quite a lot" … etc. … of private students. Also, when you describe your following at Golden Bridge, I seem to recall you sometimes say "a few people who follow me/my classes."

As I'm sure you know, it'll feel really phony at first, especially if this is what you really think/feel about it, but the "fake it till you make it" comes in handy here, I think. And sooner or later, the Universe will start hearing your change of words (connected to thoughts/feelings), too!

Hope I've somehow helped. It's just something I noticed because of your question. Again, it was soooooo good to see you. Have a great week, and thank you for being such a tremendously positive influence in my life. I'll miss you when you leave … to go to your prosperous and magnificent and successful and lucrative retreat house!!!!! :)

Sincerely, sincerely, sincerely,
Katrina (highly paid lawyer at the time she wrote this who herself went on a quest for a few years as many seekers do, leaving careers and marriages etc)

And then the follow up:

Changing the words is just an exercise in being present (difficult!) to what you're saying so you can inhibit yourself from saying words that you don't want to be putting out there. But yes, I think the more difficult task is to delve deeply into the belief system that's giving rise to the words and asking the difficult question of why that belief system is in place so you can change it internally (and the external will follow). I've been witness to your Magnificence, Donna (Sat Nam!!!) … there's just an underlying belief system that may be getting in the way sometimes.

What I have been teaching for twenty-six years is something I need to still make daily conscious efforts to practice. *Newsweek* had an article about the "Narcissistic Yoga Instructor"; my mantra has become that I need to be self-centered in order to be self-CENTERED. When a teacher comes off as though they know it all, run the other way. Yogi Bhajan taught us that we know from within; teachers only guide us there.

A beautiful young Asian girl came up to me after a class recently and said, "I want to thank you. Now I know that the answers are within me."

In Yogi Bhajan's language, this would be that we are finite but we can connect to the infinite at any time. We are all part of it. And I learn from my students, as they learn from me. To some I am transparent. They know I struggle, too. As Renee, the fabulous social worker roommate from 1997 to 2002, wrote me when she moved out (after Kent moved in in 2001), it is also working on one's self with total dedication, which she said she had never seen anyone do as devotedly as I did.

"To thine own self be true."
—Shakespeare

The challenge of the external sounds has been solved for now, yet the internal thoughts and voices are still there to learn to quiet and be with; this is so much a part of yoga practice. Weigh the negative and positive to find your neutral mind.

"The moment we have the spirit of the practice, our own discipline for ourselves, we are the incarnation of God. Then, we don't need anybody. Our purity and piety has come home."
—Yogi Bhajan

Insurmountable sounds conquered, financial fears for the time being resolved, the internal sounds of anxiety and fear receded for the moment as I focused on moving ahead.

180

Chapter 26
WIND

"A nation that destroys its soils destroys itself. Forests are the lungs of our land, purifying the air and giving fresh strength to our people."
—Theodore Roosevelt

"Prayer is the only power we have. It is my personal individual belief that prayer can change the universe. Politics and power cannot."
—Yogi Bhajan

■ Life on Mattawamkeag Changed Forever

September 2011, on a particularly luscious morning, Kent steers the old fourteen-foot aluminum fishing boat up across the open lake after one of our rare nights at the cabin. My heart wells up with the utter beauty of the place, with the joy of the privilege to experience this moment surrounded by abounding nature and beauty. My heart feels like a balloon swollen with life. The words to a yoga song come to me, and I sing them softly to myself with the only other sound the twenty-horsepower outboard motor: "This life of mine has been blessed" could not express any better my exact sentiment at this moment.

Within days, the balloon is burst by an e-mail from a man named John Gates, whom I had met previously when he stopped to introduce himself, curious about what we were doing at Sewall House. He was from Connecticut, lived in Southern Maine, and owned property nearby. His e-mail pushes my life in a direction as unexpected as many of the changes in my past, toward a new and disturbing passion. I would be fighting for the place most precious to me on earth.

I had heard about the thirty-four wind turbines (you could hardly call it a "farm" in this county, where *dairy* and *potato* usually precede the word). My mother-in-law, visiting from Sweden, this time after she retired to help with the retreat gardens and cleaning, had gone to view the objects lying on the ground a few years back with a local friend. At least, I thought—truly not giving it *much* thought—they were in the next town, not ours.

John's e-mail changed that perception. Those wind turbines had never gone up. Instead, fifty are now planned. They are larger; they are, in fact, huge, 450 feet tall, the size of a forty-five-story skyscraper. Eighty percent of Lake Mattawamkeag would view them, with red flashing lights at night. One of the most spectacular places in the country to star-gaze (nearby Baxter State Park has been ranked one of the top 5 places to see stars in the country) would be ruined, looking and sounding like an airport, with low-frequency noise emitted as well as a sound like an airplane about to take off, an intermittent whirring as the blades turned creating their *whoosh-whoosh*. I discover that eagles are attracted to the blades, their necks or wings broken or their bodies chewed up. Worse yet— the eagles become paralyzed, unable to reach their young, dying a slow and miserable death as their babies starve in the nest. Bats, already endangered by a mysterious white-nose fungal disease, do not even have to touch the blades: Their lungs burst if they are even in the vicinity of the 150-mph winds off the industrial turbines. The machines also cause Wind Turbine Syndrome, caused by low-frequency noise creeping into the walls so people cannot sleep, something the industry denies but I find to be true in during my research, meeting people affected by it here in Maine.

A 2008 guest editorial in *Environmental Health Perspectives*, published by the National Institute of Environmental Health Sciences, the US National Institutes of Health, stated: "Even seemingly clean sources of energy can have implications on human health. Wind energy will undoubtedly create noise, which increases stress, which in turn increases the risk of cardiovascular disease and cancer."

The Japanese Environment Ministry will begin a "major study into the influence of sounds of wind turbines on people's health" in April 2010, because "people living near wind power facilities are increasingly complaining of health problems." They plan a four-year examination of all 1,517 wind turbines in the country…

Our lakes, which provided healing to an ailing Theodore Roosevelt, a safe haven for beaver, deer, moose, eagles, and loons and rich habitat for song birds and other animals, to be despoiled.

In my fifty-seven years, I feel like I have never been faced so personally with anything as evil, awful, destructive as this. I wish that Stephen King (who lives in Bangor) would write about its awfulness. Intelligent liberals like him are duped by the hysterical cries of the "green machine," a lying, deceitful *greed* machine, not green at all. The book *Fire Them All* describes the corruption. We are the David against the Goliath of wind lies that run deep politically, Obama talking in each speech about the green wind industry, jobs in wind, pushing for them as a way to help our economy and environment; neither is true. I learn quickly about the existing wind warriors in the State of Maine:

- Monique, a retired physician from Belgium, as passionately in love with Maine's nature as I, heads the online Wind Task Force of less than 500 people.

- David, a young Maine Guide not unlike my great-grandfather, whose livelihood depends on the woods and the habitat remaining unspoiled.

- Gary, a feisty Queens import of many years, a dentist whose cabin and home in Lincoln have been negatively impacted by the light and noise; he is well informed on the tactics of the wind companies.

- Vic, a local man, an ex Navy Seal, fighting wind in his nearby town before I knew of this, brings me a folder full of his research and actions he has already taken.

- Plus the over 1000 on the Facebook page called Maine Wind Concerns.

Our hands are tied by an immoral law thrown in quickly by Governor Baldacci in 2008 called the Expedited Wind Law—operative word: *expedited*. With research, I learn that both of the lakes in Island Falls are highly ranked by the State of Maine, a state where preservation, conservation, and appearance have always been important. My heart hopes that their highly ranked status and the history of our area stand for something. Maine is the state that does not allow billboards on its scenic highways. This is a state that prides itself on tourism, people drawn by the natural, unspoiled beauty.

The more I learn, the less power we have. Island Falls is remote, far from anything else industrial. (the tiny closed starch factory was the only other thing in our area remotely industrial). How could this happen? Any beautiful area that has money combined with enough intelligently informed population vetoes the idea. The adjoining town of Oakfield, ten miles from Island Falls, is tiny, financially desperate. Wind companies sneak into sparsely populated areas (on the brink of poverty) with low income residents, many already on welfare, with little education, seducing the town managers and business owners. Offering crumbs of money to these small towns and their citizens over a finite period of time, the wind companies get wealthier just by putting them up, reaping major benefits from government loans and tax credits. Few people realize that our federal taxes in this time of recession are going toward these useless projects. People are bought off in secret: Once they receive the bribe monies from wind companies, the citizens accepting the bribes sign contractual gag agreements stating they can say nothing negative about the wind companies, nor sue them if they get ill or have any other issue with them. They are silenced; if they regret their decision, they have no recourse.

I have never been a political activist, not even registered to vote until I was in my thirties. Even though illnesses, natural disasters, and the powerful overcoming the weaker has always existed, this evil blindsided me.

Grateful yet distraught that John sent me the e-mail, I convince my cousin Cheryl (one of Sam's daughters) and her husband, a conservative, recently retired business executive, to come with me to see the turbines in Mars Hill, a community north of us where twenty-five industrial wind turbine machines loom over people's homes and their local ski slope. Peter and Cheryl go south fifty miles to view the wind turbines in Lincoln, where thirteen lakes have turbines overlooking their shores (where Gary, the dentist from Queens, is eventually driven out, leaving Maine). Cheryl mentions the impending situation on our lakes to another woman at church who, like Cheryl, grew up in town. The woman now summers on the other lake in town Pleasant Lake. Candy is a few years older than me, the daughter of the local vet. She had come to yoga once. Through this battle, I find a new friend and ally in her. Candy sends out all our updates to our growing list, which reaches eighty, of those opposing the wind project as they become aware of the impact on their lives that these turbines would make.

Candy and I have little time before we leave Island Falls for the winter. We call a meeting with a lawyer from Bar Harbor named Lynne Williams, who has been recommended by the Maine Wind Task Force. Lynne, around my vintage, has been an activist for years. (I had been told the wind company First Wind had bought off lawyers, too, but some lawyers cannot be bought.) Lynne does not fit the mold of the buttoned-up lawyer, the ones I would see on the other side when we went to meetings and court. With her shoulder-length curly blond hair and soft feminine build, not a body that looked over-exercised, underfed, or overly tidy, Lynne does not fit the mold of other lawyers I had encountered, including those I had taught yoga to with high-profile careers in Manhattan. Lynne is one to flash a smile easily and talk like a non-calculating human being; she enjoys her food and wine. I like her. Some suggest that we hire the more expensive lawyer who had lost the case for the Land Trust. The Trust had brought Oakfield all the way to higher court before the first thirty-four turbines were permitted. (All wind cases had lost to date, all appeals by citizens in Maine— globally as well. The case argued by the Land Trust on Pleasant Lake, which would later sell out to the wind company, had been based on the negative health impacts of wind turbines. It didn't fly.] Their lawyer was more expensive than Lynne, whom we were paying with raised funds. I did not know where the funds would come from, but forward we marched.

Lynne suggests we go to the town office to get addresses of lake property owners in particular. Like all of us before we got the word, most of them did not realize the impact these skyscraper-sized industrial machines would have on them, or that they were even happening. The DEP had told us that only forty people showed up for the general meeting about the project that had been announced in the local paper. That was half the number of people in Oakfield who voted in the project (overall population a little over 700), which was to affect hundreds of people on the lakes who did not know about it or might have thought it was hopeless since the Land Trust sold out to the company they tried to stop, after losing their case. Having done their research, the wind companies were very good at sneaking in, smooth talking, and manipulating the town officers and business owners— whom people follow blindly to keep their jobs—who believe the spin, not to lessen their being enticed by the smell of money.

The town office tells me I can have the addresses for a fee of $450. Operating with no budget, Candy and I both spend around two hours writing down addresses of taxpayers who are not from town, some who are, to send our letter to. We send 150 letters.

To Whom and All Concerned:

I am writing you with my personal concern for the 50 wind turbines which will each stand 400 feet tall that are proposed to be put within 3 miles of Mattawamkeag Lake and Pleasant Lake, said to be visible from both of the Lakes in Island Falls.

The application is going up for approval on Nov. 28, 2011. Several of us who own lake property have spoken with lawyer Lynne Williams, who is an expert on this issue. There are valuable websites available which cite the visual impact, the noise impact, and the lights that disturb the dark tranquility the nights on our lakes offer.

I have spoken personally with people from both Mars Hill and Lincoln, where these disturbances have been put up already. The wind turbines are not proven to be effective and ruin the largely natural landscape, which is the richest commodity of our lakes and our town and surrounding area.

Lynne suggested that we each write the contact person at the DEP (please do it before Nov. 28) if you are from out of state, please say you bring revenue to this area through your taxes. You can add your history of coming here to enjoy your summers on the lake. Any concerns or contributions you can add will be greatly appreciated.

The creating of these turbines requires loud blasting and clear-cutting, which ruins the topography, resulting in wildlife re-treating if they are not killed. Bats, eagles, loons are all targets for the blades. Moose and deer will not stay near the vibration of noise created by these huge skyscraper-sized machines. It is sure to tamper with our ecosystem rich with wildlife.

Wind companies state their studies find no health problems, yet they ask people they bribe with monies to sign disclaimers where they are not allowed to say anything negative about the turbines OR sue them should health problems develop. Sweden has done studies which show they cause sleep disturbances, headaches, and chronic fatigue.

Industrial wind power has not been studied enough to ruin our landscape forever for very little return and energy that will not be used in Maine but sold to other states. There are many and numerous reasons to try to stop this.

Island Falls will be voting on a wind ordinance in March. Hopefully, we can keep them off Robinson Mountain; Oakfield had no ordinance. The most important thing right now is to see if Oakfield's development can be stopped. If we get far enough with this, we will go to court and need witnesses to testify on the impact these turbines will have. Maine Guides, who recently won the first step against the turbines when LURC denied the wind application at Bowers, will be an asset for our cause.

Please help us continue to fight for the peace and beauty we all enjoy and wish to preserve. I am available by phone or e-mail and can provide you with more materials, including Lynne's work on our behalf to the Department of Environmental Protection (DEP).

Thank you.
Donna Sewall Davidge
Candy Newman Rupley

There are less than 800 residents in Island Falls, 3000 taxpayers, these numbers suggesting that seventy percent own property either on one of the lakes or in the woods. How could eighty people from Oakfield (twenty opposed it) determine the fate of all these taxpayers who came to Island Falls for its pristine and historic value? I imagine these lakefront owners innocently arriving to their place of peace and tranquility, of silence and solace, to discover fifty industrial monstrosities flashing and *whooshing* at them, ruining their peace.

I send numerous letters to the DEP, including a photo of Lincoln Lake with red flashing lights reflected on the lake. On a Saturday night, my phone rings. A man from Newton, Massachusetts, introduces himself as Carl Kaestner, who owns a camp on Pleasant Lake and has received the letter. He suggests posting a petition on change.org. Bank of America had just been been stopped from creating extra charges on their credit cards by this method.

People start sending me copies of letters they have sent to the DEP, like this couple from Kansas:

Dear DEP,

I am writing in regard to the application approval of wind turbines in Aroostook County, specifically the town of Oakfield, also Island Falls. My husband and I own property on lakeshore of Pleasant Pond in Island Falls. We have spent every summer at Pleasant Pond since 1969 when we bought a lot and built our camp. We have so much enjoyed the beautiful lake and surroundings.

My husband and I have been active in the Island Falls Lakes Association since it was founded and have served as President, Secretary, water monitor, and board members for several years. We are very much concerned re: the impact that wind turbines would have on the pristine area around Pleasant Pond and Mattawamkeag Lake. The proposed Oakfield turbines would be visible from these two lakes. We have heard firsthand from residents from other wind turbine areas concerning noise and visual disturbances.

Also, we are concerned about the effect on wildlife. As volunteers for the annual Audubon Society Loon Count on Pleasant Pond, we are always hopeful for a stable loon population and new chicks! It is believed that disturbances in the area would impact this endangered species, as well as eagles, ospreys, ducks, bats (already under stress due to disease), and other birds. Wildlife on the ground would undoubtedly be affected by construction and ongoing vibration and noise of the turbines. This area is known for tourists and visitors coming to see and hunt moose, bear, partridges, etc., which brings in revenue for local businesses.

We travel from Kansas to Maine every summer to enjoy the area, and stay from June to October. On our side of the pond, there are many camp owners who come from out of state and, of course, pay taxes each year and buy supplies locally. We feel that it is very short-sighted to allow wind turbines to disturb the ecosystem near these peaceful and beautiful lakes. Neither local residents nor out-of-state property owners and visitors condone noise or visual pollution, which cannot be changed once the turbines are in place. We are hopeful that forward thinking and long-term planning will prevail to preserve Maine's natural beauty.

Sincerely,
Martin and Doris P

And a tasting of our retreat guest comments:

I recently heard the disturbing news about the proposed placement of 50 wind turbines near Lake Mattawamkeag in Aroostook County near the town of Island Falls. I'm not a resident of Maine, but I do consider the Island Falls area to be a home away from home. Each year, I spend at least a week…enjoying the natural, unspoiled beauty of this area—especially Lake Mattawamkeag's pristine views. Throughout the entire year, while living and working in the very congested corridor between New York and Philadelphia, I look forward to that one week per year when I get to enjoy one of the Northeast's final frontiers—hiking, swimming, kayaking, and relaxing in and around the lake.

When I first visited the area 5 years ago, I was struck by the indescribable beauty, the resounding quiet, and the vistas in and around Lake Mattawamkeag. I've continued to make my pilgrimage each year and hope to make this an ongoing tradition. In addition, as a yoga instructor I'm considering bringing my students to this area to study for retreat each year as well. One of the greatest natural resources and tourist attractions in this part of Maine is undoubtedly the lack of intrusive manmade structures. If this area is allowed to be disturbed by the cutting of natural forest in order to build these large structures, I fear that I may no longer find the same value in my visits to this area. Talking pure dollars and cents, during each visit to the Island Falls area, I inject an estimated $2500 into the local economy on food, lodging, gifts, fuel, and more. Each time I come to the area, I stay at the Sewall House in Island Falls and help support one of the only retreat centers of its kind in the US—a hidden gem in the Northern Maine Woods. I visit the small syrup and honey house at Spring Break in Smyrna to buy gifts for friends back home and support the local farmers. I shop at the local grocers, fill my tank at the local convenience store, visit the local gift shops, and pay entrance fees at [nearby] Baxter State Park.

In short, the beauty of this landscape attracts visitors from far and wide willing to spend money in the community to boost the economy. If the landscape in this area becomes scarred with manmade structures, I'll be less likely to travel quite so far to visit a place that won't feel much different than natural areas closer to home. If the beauty of this area remains intact, not only will I continue to spend my $2500 per year in tourism dollars in and around Island Falls, but as mentioned above, I'm going to offer my students an opportunity to join me for retreats in the area. With 6–8 students per retreat, that can mean $15–$20K in additional revenue per visit. I sincerely encourage you and all those charged to uphold the best interest of the people of Maine (and those who love to visit it) to not allow this destructive plan to move forward. The historic interest of this location, as a retreat where a young Theodore Roosevelt would come to recuperate and meditate, should certainly be considered. Too often in our recent history, we've made the mistake of mortgaging the abundance of natural and historic splendor we've been so readily gifted for the promise of a short-term gain. In this case, allowing this plan to move forward would be another such mistake. It is the most special place in the world to me, and it would be devastating to lose even an inch of its majesty. Once that majesty is gone, it is sadly gone forever.

Sincerely,
Brian J. Critchley

Dear Jessica,

I am a native of New York City who travels to Island Falls, Maine, every summer to the yoga retreat run by Donna Davidge. It's a twelve-hour trip by bus. But I feel it's well worth it for the physical, emotional, and spiritual benefits offered by this wonderful place. Staying on the lake, hearing the loons at night, watching the sunset over the lake and the moon over the lake at night. (One particular summer evening, I thought I was looking at the set of *Swan Lake*, it was so breathtakingly beautiful!!) Walking through the forest, observing deer and moose, and then reaching Bible Point, where Theodore Roosevelt prayed, and using the Bible kept in a box on the wooden stand there to also pray. The richness of this is incalculable. And all of [a billionaire's] money could not buy it.

So I am greatly anguished to discover there is the looming danger of wind turbines which would destroy one of the few places left where one could escape "civilization" with all its ugliness, at least for a while. But enough to replenish one's spirit for the year ahead. I am an environmentalist, I believe in safe and clear energy, and I believe that wind energy is the way to go to get us off oil and nuclear. But before you accuse me of wanting it both ways, let me say that a projected technology should not be used until it is ready to be used. At the present, the turbines are too large; they will completely destroy the view of the lake, looking as they do like the Martian towers in *War of the Worlds*. In a few years, the towers will become much smaller as the technology advances. The turbines are noisy; they will destroy the serenity of this unspoiled wilderness area. Again, if you just wait a few years, more advanced and better turbines will be silent. And they kill birds and scare away wildlife. Can't we just wait a few years? What's the hurry? Unless it's someone wanting to make a buck (at the expense of a whole community and a whole ecosystem), or the result of political contributions. I would like not to be cynical and hope that that's not the case. I trust in your good will, Jessica, to think seriously about this matter. Please work to prevent this ecological carnage.

Peter Von Berg

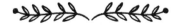

And my favorite of the many pleas sent to the DEP:

Dear DEP,

Regarding the Oakfield Wind Project, I have already expressed my concerns founded on the numerous negative effects that will most certainly take place if this project is completed. Those concerns along with the concerns written in letters from dozens of intelligent, hardworking, family-oriented, nature-loving **Americans** who purchased property, inherited land, or visit and vacation on and around Pleasant and Mattawamkeag Lakes have obviously been hastily brushed aside because the driving factor behind this project is greed and corruption. This is **EVIDENT** in the tone and bias projected in the **Draft Evergreen Wind Power II**…from the Maine DEP. Most explicitly prejudiced are the "findings" by Mister "P" (pp. 19–28) and the absolute joke of a report that he submitted. I could continue on about the inaccuracies, discrepancies, and avoidance of truths, but that is useless because we all know this project's money trail runs deep and wide with too many politicians, lobbyists and crooked businessmen with too much to gain. Either your department is powerless or in their pockets as well. Someday the truth may come out.

So, Jessica or whoever the decision makers at the DEP are, at the very least know this...

Know that you had a chance to really make a positive impact on a cause whose intentions are purely GOOD and JUST—for the existence of a place that is so serene and filled with natural beauty that hundreds of people around the country have been touched by its aura and find solace in this area. These feelings are reflected in petitions and letters sent to you and other State Agencies. This is a place that even though it is not rated by some bureaucratic organization as **Outstanding** still is (for now anyway) considered by those who have visited here **surreal**. The people whose lives YOU are affecting range from newborns being "baptized" by the clean, natural, sparkling waters of the lakes for the first time to elderly people who wish to spend their remaining precious times here and everyone in between, please know that you had the chance to maintain this place's purity and truly affect their way of life. You have the opportunity to **PROTECT AN ENVIRONMENT** [which] so many of these good people have fallen in love with and chosen as our ideal spot to rest, play, work, live, and even die. If some of us could only be so fortunate to be faced with such an opportunity. You may want to revisit the core beliefs your "Department" was founded on.

Instead, you are like a bystander watching a bully on a playground and doing nothing about it.

By choosing to issue this permit to a greedy, sneaky, multimillion-dollar conglomerate of money-hungry bullies, you are carving into virgin ground and forever altering a piece of heaven. Know that tonight you could have gone to sleep telling yourself that today you made a positive impact in an area in Southern Aroostook County. Today there are happy families and friends who will forever appreciate what you did and will celebrate, respect, and toast to you. Unfortunately, by granting this permit, you won't know this feeling. I imagine there is a part of you that feels shame. So when you go to sleep tonight, maybe you can convince yourself that somehow you did the right thing?? That in the big picture this was the right decision?? How long do you plan to fool yourself for? We have said all we can and have fought the good fight. I guess sometimes the bad guys win.

Come up to Camp Roosevelt on Pleasant Lake and visit sometime. Ask for Brian. Take a rowboat out about a mile and a half toward Sand Cove. Look northeast to the hills just to the right of the Lane Homestead and take in the view. I hear it's heavenly—for now anyway.

With sincere disappointment,
Brian M

Five hundred people signed Carl's online petition by the deadline, which the DEP extended a month. We were optimistic. We got over 200 more signatures, nearly 100 letters, and as many comments on the petition before the new January third deadline.

In November, Kent and I attended the Tax Increment Financing (TIF) meeting in Oakfield, seeing the brainwash in action. The financing was voted in, despite Maine Guide David Corrigan speaking about the wind company scams, Gary the dentist from Lincoln standing up to say how weak the finances of the company were—only to have people throw little balls of paper at him as they booed him. A Vietnam veteran named Lenny from Lincoln said the company had trespassed on his land, doing nothing to compensate him for the damages done. The seventeen complainers in Mars Hill after the turbines went up were silenced with a purported $75,000 in payouts. The money would not make the noise that made them unable to sleep stop. Mike Dicenso, who worked in the local factory in Lincoln, stood up with a photo of the red lights flashing over the lake at night, saying his taxes had gone up despite this.

The wind executives smirked, the lawyer assured the crowd with his smooth talk, the town manager and local business owner, whom I had heard had already gained by the wind company's presence (there were rumors that the town manager had a new truck and higher pay) egged the support on.

The DEP rubber-stamped the project, their title "Environmental Protection" a sad oxymoron.

My nights were consumed with hot-flash awakenings, haunted with the vision of these deceptive wind executives, and their flashing skyscraper sized machines, plugging these invasive industrial machines. Keeping abreast of developments, reports worldwide and locally, by the Wind Task Force, a group called Long Islander (one anonymous person on top of every development and article in Maine as it came out), Save the Eagles (out of Europe), Wind Watch.org and the North American Platform Against Wind all shared articles we could comment on. Comment I did a plenty; I rallied on.

A journalist at the Bangor Daily News contacted me, saying we were overly sensitive to noise. "Hey, look," he said, "people live on the Long Island Expressway"—his ignorant, arrogant comment. Northern Mainers chose to live where they did for a reason, as well as the people who chose to own property here for the summer months.

Environmental organizations that should have been fighting against the wind turbines—the Natural Resources Council of Maine, Audubon, and the Sierra Club—jumped on the lying bandwagon, receiving purported donations from wind companies. While in Europe, electricity prices skyrocket because of it; the cries of reduced CO_2 emissions while toxins are created by the production of these monstrous turbines from China and Europe; mass destruction of acres of virgin forests and natural habitat to erect these penile symbols in the sky—the scam marched on. Each turbine runs on 400 gallons of oil, the claim being they would get us off oil. We appealed the DEP, then the BEP, but both rubber-stamped it. Not one case in the State of Maine had won. One upcoming case looked promising, even as ours had in moments, but the spread continued like a virus.

I wrote TV journalists, well known documentary film makers that were known for challenging society with the truth, and a well known anti oil activist, who sent no reply but put me on his anti-oil e-mail list without my permission. No one responded. We had a guest for two nights in May 2012 who had been a producer at *60 Minutes*. She suggested I try this approach again. I wrote the journalists once again to no avail.

The scenic specialist for the State who had been at the BEP appeal in April admitted he had no accurate standard for scenic assessment, even though a scenic specialist from Vermont I had spoken with in the beginning of the battle had suggested that anything within eight miles (the turbines were a mile and half to three miles away from some parts of the lakes) was an issue. The BEP implied that our area, because it was low-income, low-education, and low-population, did not matter when the question arose about the influx of people between May and September. The appeal to the higher court had not stopped one project to date. Forever ruined, these once pristine parts of Maine will no longer live up to the State's tagline, "Maine, the way life should be."

TR, who fought so hard for conservation and wildlife and to prevent blasting of hilltops for mining in places like Alaska, is turning over in his grave. How I wish I could extract his spirit to give us more power to fight the Goliath of corporate greed.

Every rose has its thorn.
Every summer has its fall.
Every winter has its spring.
Like the sun has its rain.
> —Kent Bonham (my second husband)

Wind was a concept my mother had to consider if we were going to take the silver aluminum clunker canoe out on the lake or if we were to take the fourteen-foot aluminum boat on the lake to go the fifteen to twenty- minute boat ride to town to get supplies. We had to keep an eye on the weather to see if the wind was bringing in a fast thunderstorm, in which case our boat became a lightning rod. My mother instilled the fear of God in us about taking the boats out in lightning or even if it looked like there might be the *possibility* of lightning, which could come up fast. Other than storms, the high winds mostly occurred in autumn when we were back in school.

Sometimes, lying in the quiet, the dead quiet of night, at the cabin five miles away from anything and anyone, I could hear the wind rustling in the trees. It was a beautiful sound, reassuring and haunting at the same time. When my mother, in her eighties, hinted that she might sell the log cabin, I whispered to her, "Please, no, Mom, that place is my soul." To me, in that moment, my normally loud voice sounded like those rustling leaves moving gently in the wind, watching me in the early morning, warning me in the afternoon if I had to move the boat into the cove to keep it from slamming on the rocky shore in front of the cabin as we slept at night. It must have relieved my mother to know that one of her offspring cared about her cabin as much as she did. She kept the cabin, leaving it to me and my sister in her will. Our relationship was a complicated one, but this one thing created a bond, even if the bond felt distant—a love for nature, for Maine, for the healing spirituality her cabin and this lake provided. My sister, long since escaped to California, moving there right after attending college at Northwestern, never returned east except for visits. My brother, after being institutionalized for his mental problems in the 1960's, would never function in the "real" world, transitioning to a halfway house in Hartford, ending up back with my parents, who later bought him his own condo as they approached the inevitable. I was the one to relish the cabin whenever I could.

Who would have thought, when I took the leap of faith to purchase my great-grandparents' homestead "uptown," that the wind would become my enemy? Not the wind, exactly, but the people who greedily claimed they could use this intermittent energy source to create electricity for people outside of Maine, outside of our state. (even for the out of Staters, the amount of energy produced was miniscule) What sense did that make? To blast our hills, to kill and scare off our wildlife, to ruin our topography—which Henry David Thoreau and Theodore Roosevelt had written about, the Maine woods—forever? Who would have thought, when I decided to make the leap of faith to create a retreat for weary city dwellers—a place where the industrialized views and sounds of progress were so very far away that people always commented, "I had no idea you were so far away from everything" and "It took forever to get here, but boy, was it worth it"—that we would be fighting this wind battle?

Fifteen years into putting our all into it, with people coming from across the country and a spattering from other countries—England, Finland, Holland—the retreat was working despite my uncertainty. My Swedish husband and I had kept it going. Positive reviews continued to come in from the press, also from individuals via Trip Advisor and the more recent Google Listing. Season by season we were keeping it going, putting most of the income into improving it, bit by bit making it better and better for our guests, people seeking silence, beauty, and solace in their lives. Through some good fortune, they found it with us.

Things come in threes. I thought nothing could be more challenging than our experiences with the starch factory and the local bar. What were the odds of such disturbances in this quiet hamlet off the beaten path, population less than 800? It existed as a place back in time, people waving at you as they took their daily walk or drove by, friendly hellos at the post office, small talk about the weather, always something to watch in a beautiful nature-filled spot like Island Falls. My great-grandparents had settled here for the beauty of the location, a tiny island sandwiched between the rushing river water we called "the falls." Where the first Sewall home had been just opposite the falls was now the Briar Patch Gift and Flower shop, one of the few businesses still struggling to survive in Island Falls (since closed). A painting of the first Sewall house, a log cabin, hung next to the fireplace in the living room at our Sewall House, one of many contents that called me to reflect on the people and life of the past in the home and in this little town.

Blindsided, this never-changing simplicity was challenged by a destruction I could never have fathomed, especially so far from so much. My heart felt cracked every day, as many other hearts had cracked in Lincoln, where Mt. Katahdin and a number of lakes now saw and heard the invader of the peace. The wind "energy" atrocity was greed, not green. (see the documentary WINDFALL for more on this).

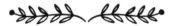

"If future generations are to remember us with gratitude rather than contempt, we must leave them something more than the miracles of technology. We must leave them a glimpse of the world as it was in the beginning, not just after we got through with it."

—President Lyndon Johnson
on signing the Wilderness Act of 1964

■ January 3, 2012: Premonition of Things to Come

The alarm gongs lightly, but I had not set it. My husband sleepily says turn it off, explaining he must have accidentally set it: "Push the button on the right." I do. It gongs again five minutes later. "No, the *big* button on the right. You are so inept."

His condescending harshness in his matter-of-fact Swedish voice cuts to all my feeling of hurt, inadequacy, and, no matter how much I try, not getting where I had hoped to be. Strange dreams come in of Katy Holmes and Tom Cruise, recently divorced…his control of her as I try to get to her… Is my dream a metaphor? A message?

Last night I was trying to scan a copy of my master's degree for some online listing, but I could not remember which cord to take from the modem to the printer. "I showed you that already." In that same parental *you are stupid* tone. What am I inept at? Living. Sometimes I am in awe of life; sometimes I wish I were never born or could stop trying and go away forever, those moments fluttering a thought in my mind: Just let it be the end. Of what?

"There are, it seems, two muses: the Muse of Inspiration, who gives us inarticulate visions and desires, and the Muse of Realization, who returns again and again to say, "It is yet more difficult than you thought." This is the muse of form. It may be then that form serves us best when it works as an obstruction, to baffle us and deflect our intended course. It may be that when we no longer know what to do, we have come to our real work, and when we no longer know which way to go, we have begun our real journey. The mind that is not baffled is not employed. The impeded stream is the one that sings."

—Wendell Berry

■ **January 3, 2014**

In the end only three things matter—
How much you loved
How gently you lived
How gracefully you let go of things not meant for you.

> —*Dut Dut House, August 30, 2013*
> *the name for my mother's cabin that my brother,*
> *who was 2 at the time, called it as he listened to my*
> *mother's cousin Sam and his father Merrill*
> *hammer the cabin into place as they built it.*

Despite All—Nature Heals

Every time I step out into the utter silence to see the clearest star-filled sky one can imagine, I suffer the sting of yet one more mosquito biting the top of my bare feet. How luscious the earth is, how my bites burn! A rare night at the cabin alone, some mysterious thumping noise off in the distance interrupting the silence—wood being chopped at 9 p.m.? Fireworks? Early sleep befalls me, as it does here in safety and seclusion. I think even death would not scare me here. I understand how my mother made such an effort to be assisted up the rocky shore, oxygen tank in tow, the August before her death in April 2004. Perhaps she hoped to face death in this peaceful place, to make the natural transition here surrounded by nature, which is what we go back to anyway.

I have awoken after a night of intermittent rain on the metal roof. First dip in the cool lake— cool water because, after all, tomorrow is September—feeling the grasses growing unrevealed in the water until they massage my legs as I swim. Coffee in the percolator on the ancient propane stove, three burners on iron legs placed on the counter—the same one my mother used—the first thing popping into my mind as I look at the lake, "Thank you, Mom." Did I ever say that enough when she was alive? She thought I was difficult and selfish; my younger husband accused me of the same. Do we continue to attract the wound? Such thoughts prevail despite the cleansing feeling of my first night alone at the cabin all summer, Sewall House obligations constantly calling on my attention and energies.

I reflect on a yoga teaching job I may be losing after nearly twenty-five years in my freelance world. I look at the serene lake and ask myself, "If I were to die tomorrow, or today, for that matter, where would I rather be?" The answer has no hesitation though the reality of bill-paying prevails.

Despite the book about finances I have kept that my father gave me in 1998, which says save, save, save, I cannot blame my husband, though I would like to, for the fact that we have put our all into Sewall House, the rich experiences and challenges having no measure in a retirement account. The life of the artist, as my mother called me, entails risks. Life entails risks.

I walk outside to wash the top of the percolator in the lake, discovering a heart-shaped pink mushroom, which I shoot a photo of with my phone. I come back inside the old cabin to place its keys in the pocket of the purple Patagonia pullover fleece given to me twenty years ago by the boyfriend I trekked Nepal with. In this moment, life and its memories are good.

Last week, the little mouse that drowned in the dishwater left overnight for the poor creature to fall into, saddened me, reminding me of the childhood mouse I gave a funeral for in a matchbox in our backyard. I ask myself, "Does that compassion toward living creatures sound like the selfishness my mother, and now my husband, say I have, or do the world's projections onto us test us to make us doubt our good?

Forest Bathing

"The Japanese term Shinrin-yoku may literally mean "forest bathing," but it doesn't involve soaking in a tub among the trees. Rather it refers to spending time in the woods for its therapeutic (or bathing) effect. Most of us have felt tension slip away in the midst of trees and nature's beauty. But science now confirms its healing influence on the body. When you spend a few hours on a woodland hike or camping by a lake, you breathe in phytoncides, active substances released by plants to protect them against insects and from rotting, which appear to lower blood pressure and stress and boost your immune system."

—Mother Nature Network

Chapter 27
ANOTHER SNOWY DAY, 2014

Another snowy day much like the day Aunt Nancy passed away in 1996. New York City has an eerie quietness as I nurse the cough in my chest that approached my body as it usually does, a scratchy throat night before last that made sleep a challenge. Finally I resort to a natural sleeping remedy called Tranquil, which Kent discovered in his quest for equilibrium and which I have used on occasion since the inception of menopausal sleep since 2009. He is holed up in the subzero temperatures of Maine once again in winter, this time colder than other winters, this coldness having crept into our relationship for the last year. Signs of it were there two years ago when the returning guest who loved us both left me a small gift and a note upon her departure: "Dear Donna, I had a wonderful time. Thank you for sharing your beautiful home. You are very special and I am glad you are in my life. Kent is fabulous also, but I hope he knows how very lucky he is. I'll be back again." She never returns.

This past summer was more of this. On the third day, our young chef (we had found on short notice when Kent decided he did not want to chef - she turned out to be brilliant) pulled me aside and said, "I respect you and your husband. I need you to know that if you want to ask him to leave, I will not leave you." The incident two years ago that precipitated the note the guest had left me upon her departure had been during a full yoga class at Sewall House. Class was full, one of my training graduates from Canada vacationing in the area stopping by to join the class while two trainers and four guests were also present. I was moving with joy to the yoga music as I taught. Kent approached the stereo, tore the music off, then turned his venom on me with a stern tone: "Yoga teachers do not act like that."

A young woman, a repeat guest who had come with her mother her first visit, this time bartering with us to unclutter our personal space, which sorely needed it, received all of Kent's attention that week, snickering as he removed the music. (When she moves a personal item of mine from our space without my consent, I find it in the kitchen and ask her why she moved it. She becomes hurt by my confrontation. She asks to have a session with me and Kent to speak about her feelings. In the session, Kent angrily blurts out that I am jealous of her because she is young and beautiful. She suggests that Kent look at me, saying his comment calls for therapy, something beyond her scope as a "declutterer." It seems our relationship is becoming the mess.)

Two years later, when Kent finds us a pleasant female therapist in Maine, an hour's drive from Sewall House, as many things are, the chef has already approached me with her offer of staying if I ask him to go. Kent is cold and hostile in front of guests the entire retreat season. The husband who used to be my loving counterpart is gone. The therapist patiently asks him if he realizes the meds he has been on since the spring are a controlled substance, something he was addicted to in his early twenties, which he says make him "normal." His has self-diagnosed himself, pronouncing that he has ADHD, finding a nurse practitioner online that prescribes the amphetamines. The hostility and anger I had seen intermittently and infrequently over the past couple of years becomes a constant edge now that he is on these drugs, me wondering when he will go over the edge again. Now, on January 3rd, we cannot have a conversation without his saying I am controlling, bickering.

His irrationality spills over into things like telling me we have been hacked, not to use my computer or cell phone, to discontinue the e-mail account I have had for years. He accuses me of having sex outside the marriage, that I lie, cheat, and withhold money. He says he does not own half of the house, even as he bullied me for two days last spring to bring forth the papers to prove that I had signed half of Sewall House over to him, which I did in 2005 at his request, ten days before his first relapse. He says he has been unhappy since 2005. I consult a lawyer that my father's lawyer finds for me. I can hardly believe I am watching this marriage unravel. As Kent is approaching fifty, I suggest it may be a midlife crisis, which angers him the way everything I say does. I speak with his mother in Sweden, who says his father also got angry with everything until, having waited too long, she divorced him.

It is a cold day in New York, colder in Island Falls; I am comforted by my work, by the students I love, who appreciate me even as they suffer their own challenges and know nothing of mine. I am comforted that my father is alive, though forgetful, knowing he will not be there much longer as my lifeline, my eternal support, the one who waited up for me at night, who begged me not to leave my first marriage. I reflect, seeing the wisdom of a parent's love.

I live the moments, taking the train in from my father's on New Year's Day, arriving at Grand Central, realizing I have time to walk the two miles from 42nd to 86th Street to teach the 9 a.m. class at PURE Yoga. I am subbing there for a power yoga class, wondering who will show, what strangers I will teach on this first day of the year; the city is so still. I take a moment to look back at Grand Central as I walk up the stairs to the exit; I pause and snap a photo of Grand Central asleep but bright on the morning after the mayhem I gladly missed. A police officer completes the snapshot, making it all the more New York-ish because he is in it with his cup of coffee. He turns away, but I have already snapped the picture. Did he turn away because he thought of something taking him in the opposite direction, or because he did not want to be in the shot? I will never know.

I turn around, enter the cold crisp air of the sunny first day of 2014, headed up Park Avenue with the few others strolling. The clock in the photo is at 7:45, time stopped but only on camera. In reality, it marches on. As I get closer to my destination, there are coffee shops and cafés open along Madison Avenue, a homeless person asleep sitting up in a doorway, covered completely by a blanket. I do not know if it is a male or female. I turn back, as I did to take the photo at Grand Central, to dig five dollars from my purse and lay it in the person's bag next to the empty bottle sticking out of the top of it. I wonder if they will lurch out at me, crazy person that they might be, but they do not budge. The snow will fall in three days, when I write this page. I wonder where the homeless will go then.

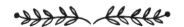

"In the sadness of deep loss lies a more open heart. As if the tears fertilize the crevices and cracks so that when you think your heart is broken, it is actually being watered for more growth — even the pain distills."

The above quote was written by me on May 2, 2014, en route to Theodore Roosevelt's Oyster Bay Long Island home, on the train, a day after the town of Oakfield got their stinking money for the wind turbines.

Chapter 28
MY FATHER'S FEET

■ **November 1, 2014**

As I gaze at his distorted feet, I know he will leave me, not intentional-
ly, because we never want to leave each other, but so it goes. His tiny
body still walking along, now with a cane, even with the right knee that
sticks out further than a wishbone, also distorted by gradual expression

of an injury from thirty years ago—the map of our bodies, the image of our self.

I, too, have the same distorted feet, forty years younger, and the same lump of fat deposited on my also thin inner left forearm. We are blueprints of each other. What shall I ever do without him? My anchor, my guide, my unconditional love. The room encompasses me, the quiet of it, the comfort of it, the clutter of it, the latter a trait we share, too. Could my heart ever be as large as his? I think if it were, it would burst.

I gaze at his facial skin, looking so good for someone who has lived on the planet for one hundred years. "I'm an old man," he jokes, his wit intact, his brilliant intellect intact, though he feels the slipping of his short-term memory, so common as the first thing to go.

He stares intently at the small screen in front of him, determined to repeat over and over again the lesson of modern technology he finds so challenging but is determined not to give up on. I coach him patiently, I gaze at him with amusement and love—with so much gratitude that he sits here so still involved in living, remarkably so, still caring about so much and so many.

He is my father, and when he leaves, I feel my world might end—this man who changed my diapers while my mother slept through the night, this man who chokes up at all the loving memories of his life and of mine, with any mention of his deceased beloved wife.

Together, a thing Aunt Nancy shared with us, we are the sentimentalists.

Chapter 29
KEEP ON SHOOTIN'

"Life, Death, and Violence as Viewed by William Sewall as Sheriff and in the Woods" featured in *The American Magazine*, February 1926:

Finding out in this interview that my great-grandfather became sheriff at age sixty, when the railroad came to Island Falls, and managed criminals without a gun and viewed hunting as sport not slaughter. These were my findings in the article with the above title that I finally read on my Sixtieth Birthday, giving myself silence and time to read this, which had been sitting in a cloth bag in my closet waiting to be read, found in the Sewall House library, a treasure trove of un inventoried memorabilia.

■ **January 15, 2015, My Sixtieth Birthday**
Twenty-four Hours of Silence, 4 p.m. to 4 p.m.
(Birth time January 15, 1955 4:20 pm Stamford CT)

Today on the subway to teach at the Federal Reserve Bank of NY before going on silence, I pick up a *Metro NY* free paper, reading how a well-known actress, who is playing a woman with early-onset Alzheimer's in *Almost Alice* is feeling that anything we do in life doesn't matter. I get what she means, but the opposite end of that is to make the moments count because they are all *life*, which can be altered drastically or changed at any moment.

Going through things I have saved over the years of my many experiences in hopes to discern what I am trying to do with this manuscript, I find this letter from my British Shakespeare acting teacher dated "Tuesday," undoubtedly a Tuesday in the early 1990s:

Dear Donna—

This moment I have found my card from the blond Macbeths, which I kept to thank you for, I think I have, but thank you! So glad to see you again—you make us listen—the most important thing—involved—but too small and not defined in the journey. Somehow I long to be "tidy" and this needed clearing up. You have a quality I admire—in life as in work— Define—make your journey. It must communicate. You cause the audience to come to you—but you must also go out.

Love,
Ada

I destroyed this card after recording it on my sixtieth birthday, kept all these years, feel a little sad about getting rid of it.

I discover *The American Magazine* from February 1926 on my day of silence. It contains a lengthy interview with my great-grandfather, telling stories in more detail than the general things I knew about his vast knowledge at an early age about the woods and all things therein. Perhaps my love for life and nature comes from this advice from his own father, not a woodsman but a pioneer who settled Island Falls out of a need for land after his shoe business burned to the ground in Massachusetts. My great-great-grandfather's advice to his very young son, who did his first nature guiding at age ten in the thick woods of Northern Maine: "Billy, don't get scared of anything until it hurts you, and you won't get scared very often."

My great-grandfather's response at eighty-plus: "Well, I have lived in the woods all my days, and I've still to be hurt by them." I sense that his love of nature has passed to my cells. Either way, the actress is right. We all leave the planet someday, somehow. At the same time, I feel enriched by the knowledge of these ancestors I did not meet but who, through the legacy and words, I feel. My one-woman show was the beginning of this fascination through my imaginary dialogue between me and my great grandmother Mary Sewall. There is more, actually recorded, to discover about William, a uniquely rich man to learn much from, even from the grave.

A year before Theodore Roosevelt died (1918), a biographer named Herman Haggedorn interviewed him about his biography.

Roosevelt said there was one man Haggedorn had to speak to, and that was Bill Sewall, who had known him when "He had his bark on." (in his youth, before becoming a fully formed man).

Haggedorn liked what my great-grandfather had to say so much he made the interview into a book called *Bill Sewall's Story of TR*. By the end of the magazine interview, I think I know how Haggedorn biographer felt—all the detailed stories and the amazing memory of my then eighty-something-year-old ancestor in the magazine article drew me in.

His parting words in the article resonated as a metaphor for life, the defined journey my Shakespeare acting teacher Ada wrote me about: "It pays to keep on shootin', son, and give to each shot the best you can. The man who lets a miss upset him will never be a hunter. You'll miss now and then, sure as you are human. Then again, what you think is a miss may also be a hit between the eyes."

❧❧❧❧❧ ~ ❧❧❧❧❧

"I never understand when people say, 'Do you do comedy or tragedy?' I don't think they're very much different. They both have to be true, and there isn't a great play in the world that doesn't have funny parts. The whole idea is to reflect life in some way, which means surely you have to have both."

—Mike Nichols

Now I become myself. It's taken
Time, many years and places;
I have been dissolved and shaken,
Worn other people's faces,
Run madly, as if Time were there,
Terribly old, crying a warning,
"Hurry, you will be dead before-
What? Before you reach the morning?
Or the end of the poem is clear?
Or love safe in the walled city?)
Now to stand still, to be here,
Feel my own weight and density!

—From "Now I Become Myself" by May Sarton

■ **Saturday August 13 7 pm 2016 MY FINAL ENTRY**

I have just carried a pail of warm lake water up to the cabin in a red
plastic pail - warm because the lake is low and temperatures have
been high

along the short grassed path scattered with occasional rocks embedded in the earth

a path I have walked on many a summer many a time

since I was able to walk

my bare feet have a sensation of not quite tingling
of the energy of the earth grass and rock
they have just communicated with

I sweep my hand over the bottom of my foot
wondering if tics attach that quickly
not a concern in my childhood because they were not here
and still not prevalent here- yet

As I gaze now from the cabin at the lake
a feeling plunges into my hands
plunge the only word that seems correct to describe it
could be from carrying the water
but it is both hands
the onset of arthritis that time brings upon us?

creeping creeping pressing passing

FOR THIS MOMENT WE ARE HERE

EPILOGUE

*"What the caterpillar calls the end the rest of
the world call a butterfly"*
–LAO TZU

In 2014, I filed for divorce. Kent moved to Los Angeles, then to Las Vegas. Over-riding our pre-nuptial agreement, I had given him half the house but kept the actual business of Sewall House Yoga Retreat. My divorce lawyer, a kind, gentle man, suggested I freeze the business until I knew if I had to sell the house. I ran the retreat anyway, with the help of Nadja. I finally settled by buying Kent out, thus purchasing the Sewall House twice. By 2017, we had repaired the relationship enough to be friends. Kent moved back to Sweden in 2019, where he is working and strong again. We remain friends.

In 2015, the wind turbines went up over our beautiful lakes, monstrosities with red flashing lights, clear-cut land rubble where once had been hundreds of acres of pristine forest and habitat. I know Theodore Roosevelt would have opposed them, their corporate greed, lies, and deceptions. I still oppose them, involved in supporting those who suffer from them globally, as well as being on a Maine State Committee opposing Industrial Wind.

My father, at age 101, fell and broke his femur. I was asleep visiting him the night it happened in March 2016, with him both pre- and post-surgery. On the eve of Father's Day in June 2017, my father passed away at 102 years and four months of age. I was in his hospital room with him for forty-eight hours before he died, driving down to Connecticut from Sewall House. I returned to Sewall House, his last words to me "Good morning Darling". Within twenty-four hours of my return to Maine, he passed. Every day I miss the man who loved me and understood me unconditionally. I always will. My parents are buried in Island Falls.

In 2019 Z's wife of 14 years reaches out to me via Facebook message to ask if he was abusive with me, writing to me that as she has grown in her strength she realizes he has issues and feels he is abusive. I had not seen the message, sent months before, I go to her Facebook profile. It appears she has returned home with their children, though she writes he is not making it easy. Ironic I should hear from this woman as I finish the editing on this book about finding my strength as a woman out of the blue from a woman I do not know. As I say in the introduction, we are all interconnected. We can all grow stronger, help each other to do so, if only by example. And pray for change for those who suffer so much that they hurt others. As the wise man Jesus said "forgive them for they know not what they do" (no slander intended in this memoir, only my experiences as truthfully and without harm meant for anyone- stories shared to mold the story). As I do the final proof edit, Z is now back in my life, as is Kent, as a friend I am in touch with.

The adventure which is the uncertainty of life, my yoga teaching since 1985 in a world now filled with yoga, continues, as well as the uncertainty of Sewall House Yoga Retreat's future. But then what is certain? I am grateful for the students and teachers (and employers) I have learned from, who have sustained my search for answers to the question from my poem "Why." I am grateful for the yoga technology that has brought me healing through purity in mind, body and breath. And I am grateful for the legacy of my roots- and of William Windgate Sewall, who knew the power of friendship beyond boundaries, as did his friend Theodore.

TO CONCLUDE:

From Theodore Roosevelt the Fourth in an April 2017 *Bangor Daily News* editorial about the new National Monument in Northern Maine (Katahdin Woods and Waters) near Sewall House:

Many forget it was a Maine lumberman and guide, Bill Sewall, who helped shape Ted Roosevelt's love for the outdoors and for this state. Bill was massive and strong; it was as though his muscles and bones were carved from Maine's own earth. When they met, TR was a nineteen-year-old student at Harvard, asthmatic and, as Bill told it (long after TR's death), "weak." [I am adding that Arthur Cutler, the professor who sent TR north, let Bill Sewall know that TR was weak and not to push him because he would do most anything, which he did and *healed* from.]

Together they climbed Katahdin, fished, hunted, and trekked. Miles upon miles. They trekked all the way to the White House, where Bill and his wife stood next to the president on a receiving line at a reception in Bill's honor. The president and Bill knew what it took to keep going. One more step. Character and grit forged here in Maine's mountains and forests.

William Sewall (my great-grandfather), his nephew Wilmot Dow, and a young Theodore Roosevelt during a Sewall House stay.

ONLINE RESOURCES

http://bangordailynews.com/2017/04/11/opinion/contributors/te
ddy-roosevelt-would-have-had-high-hopes-for-north-woods-
monument

article on pineal gland and third eye:
http://www.ce5.be/eng/blog/?p=612

http://howgreenisthis.org/about/whats-wrong-with-industrial-wind-
turbines/

http://www.dailymail.co.uk/home/moslive/article-1350811/In-
China-true-cost-Britains-clean-green-wind-power-experiment-
Pollution-disastrous-scale.html

ONE OF THE BEST BOOKS ON YOGA I HAVE READ
and my yoga library is huge!

Eddie Stern is the Ashtanga I discovered in 1999

Recommended BOOK ON HOW YOGA WORKS/Heals by my
Ashtanga Yoga teacher Eddie Stern 2019:

ONE SIMPLE THING by Eddie Stern available for purchase online

Released shortly before this book, Eddie's book brings to light many
of the subtle messages of this memoir.

From page 52: "YOGA IN ITS MOST BASIC SENSE IS A RITU-
AL THAT WE PERFORM TO HELP US REMAIN ESTAB-
LISHED IN AWARENESS"

Yogi Bhajan Patience Pays
(AVAILABLE AS A RECORDING FROM A-Healing.com)

"Patience pays. Wait. Let the hand of God work for you. The One who has created you, let Him create all the environments, circumstances, and facilities and faculties.

Oh individual, why you are in a very doubtful state? The One who has made you will take care of you. The One who has created this Universe, all the planets, planetary faculties and facilities on Earth, He is the One who has created you. Wait. Have patience. Lean on him. And all best things will come to you.

Dwell in God. Dwell in God. Dwell in God. Befriend your soul. Dwell in God and befriend your soul. Dwell in God and befriend your soul. Dwell in God and befriend your soul. All the faculties and facilities of the Creation, which are in your best interest shall be at your feet. You need million things. Million things will reach you if you are stable, established, firm, patient. Remember, Creator watches over you and Creation is ready to serve you, if you just be you.

So please take away the ghost of your life and stop chasing round. Consolidate. Concentrate. Be you. And may all the peace and peaceful environments, prosperity approach you forever. Sat Nam"

And now, dear reader, these words I share with you are finally complete.

The grave of my great-grandfather, William Wingate Sewall.

Made in the USA
Monee, IL
04 June 2020